麦格希 中英双语阅读文库

永远的原始生活

【美】 阿妮塔·利姆 (Anita Lim) ●主编

刘思光　孔研　崔剑剑●译

麦格希中英双语阅读文库编委会●编

全国百佳图书出版单位
吉林出版集团股份有限公司

图书在版编目（CIP）数据

永远的原始生活 / (美) 阿妮塔·利姆 (AnitaLim) 主编；麦格希中英双语阅读文库编委会编；刘思光，孔研，崔剑剑译. -- 2版. -- 长春：吉林出版集团股份有限公司，2018.3（2022.1重印）
（麦格希中英双语阅读文库）
ISBN 978-7-5581-4774-6

Ⅰ.①永… Ⅱ.①阿… ②麦… ③刘… ④孔… ⑤崔… Ⅲ.①英语—汉语—对照读物②故事—作品集—美国—现代 Ⅳ.①H319.4：I

中国版本图书馆CIP数据核字(2018)第046092号

永远的原始生活

编：	麦格希中英双语阅读文库编委会
插　画：	齐　航　李延霞
责任编辑：	欧阳鹏
封面设计：	冯冯翼
开　本：	660mm×960mm　1/16
字　数：	220千字
印　张：	9.75
版　次：	2018年3月第2版
印　次：	2022年1月第2次印刷

出　版：	吉林出版集团股份有限公司
发　行：	吉林出版集团外语教育有限公司
地　址：	长春市福祉大路5788号龙腾国际大厦B座7层
	邮编：130011
电　话：	总编办：0431-81629929
	发行部：0431-81629927　0431-81629921(Fax)
印　刷：	北京一鑫印务有限责任公司

ISBN 978-7-5581-4774-6　　　定价：35.00元

前言 *PREFACE*

英国思想家培根说过：阅读使人深刻。阅读的真正目的是获取信息，开拓视野和陶冶情操。从语言学习的角度来说，学习语言若没有大量阅读就如隔靴搔痒，因为阅读中的语言是最丰富、最灵活、最具表现力、最符合生活情景的，同时读物中的情节、故事引人入胜，进而能充分调动读者的阅读兴趣，培养读者的文学修养，至此，语言的学习水到渠成。

"麦格希中英双语阅读文库"在世界范围内选材，涉及科普、社会文化、文学名著、传奇故事、成长励志等多个系列，充分满足英语学习者课外阅读之所需，在阅读中学习英语、提高能力。

◎难度适中

本套图书充分照顾读者的英语学习阶段和水平，从读者的阅读兴趣出发，以难易适中的英语语言为立足点，选材精心、编排合理。

◎精品荟萃

本套图书注重经典阅读与实用阅读并举。既包含国内外脍炙人口、耳熟能详的美文，又包含科普、人文、故事、励志类等多学科的精彩文章。

◎功能实用

本套图书充分体现了双语阅读的功能和优势，充分考虑到读者课外阅读的方便，超出核心词表的词汇均出现在使其意义明显的语境之中，并标注释义。

鉴于编者水平有限，凡不周之处，谬误之处，皆欢迎批评教正。

我们真心地希望本套图书承载的文化知识和英语阅读的策略对提高读者的英语著作欣赏水平和英语运用能力有所裨益。

丛书编委会

Contents

01

Native Americans of the Great Plains

The Great Plains

The Great Plains of the United States stretch from the Rocky Mountains in the west beyond the Missouri River in the east. The Great Plains extend north into Canada and south nearly to Mexico.

Long ago the Great Plains were *characterized* by gently rolling hills covered with tall grasses. With few trees to block them, strong winds

---

大平原上的美洲原住民

大平原

美国大平原西起落基山脉，向东越过密苏里河，北抵加拿大境内，南至墨西哥边界。

很久以前，大平原以被高茂的草地覆盖着的平缓起伏的丘陵为主。这里几乎没有树木遮挡，疾风扫过大平原，夏天吹来热风，而到了冬天，

---

characterize *v.* 以……为特征

whipped across the Great Plains, blowing hot in the summer and bitterly cold in the winter. It was dry, with *rainfall* averaging 20 inches (51 cm) a year.

A little over two hundred years ago, in the early 1800s, there were only 150,000 people living in the Great Plains. Most were Native Americans, but there were also European settlers.

People shared the Great Plains with more than sixty million *bison*, or buffalo. Bison were the *mainstay* of many Plains tribes' diets, which meant that as the animals migrated, or moved with the seasons, many of the tribes moved with them. As you read about the people who lived on the Great Plains, you'll see how they depended on the bison for more than food.

却变成了刺骨的寒风。这里很干燥，年平均降水量只有20英寸（51厘米）。

200多年前，在19世纪早期，只有15万人居住在大平原上。大部分的居民为美洲原住民，但也有欧洲殖民者。

人们与6000多万头北美野牛（或叫作水牛）共同分享这片大平原。北美野牛是大平原各部落饮食中的主要来源，它们随着季节迁徙，野牛迁徙到哪里，很多部落也会迁徙到哪里。如果你读过关于生活在大平原上人们的故事，你就会知道野牛对他们的意义不仅仅局限于食物。

---

rainfall *n.* 降雨量

mainstay *n.* 支柱

bison *n.* 野牛

Tribes of the Plains

There are more than thirty tribes that make up the Plains Native Americans. The tribes of the Great Plains all have different languages and customs, but they also have much in common based on geography.

Home on the Plains

Lots of people think of *teepees* as typical homes for Native Americans of the past, and many Plains tribes actually did live in teepees. These amazing mobile homes were ideal for *nomadic* hunters on the Plains because they were designed to be strong enough to *withstand* heavy winds, provide heat in the winter, and let air flow through in the hot summer months.

平原部落

大平原上有三十多个部落，这些部落组成了大平原上的美洲原住民。平原部落有各自的语言和习俗，但基于地理因素，他们还是有很多共同之处的。

大平原上的家园

很多人认为圆锥形帐篷是过去美洲原住民特有的住所，很多平原部落确实也住在圆锥形帐篷里。这些让人惊异的移动家园对大平原上的游牧猎人来说是非常理想的，因为它们被设计得足够结实以致能够抵挡大风，在冬季能够防寒，夏季也能够使空气流通。

---

teepee *n.* 圆锥形帐篷　　　　　　　　nomadic *adj.* 游牧的
withstand *v.* 经受住

Wood poles gave the teepee its cone shape, and some of the poles were 25 feet (7.6 m) tall. Bison *hides* were *stitched* together to make the walls. The poles and hides that made the teepee could be quickly taken down and then transported to a new location. Once a tribe decided where to settle, two to three people could set up a teepee in less than two hours.

A large family could *comfortably* live in a teepee, which had a living area about 15 feet (4.57 m) in *diameter*, with enough room to cook during the day and sleep at night. The door, or opening, often faced east because there was less wind coming from the east. When cooking or heating the inside, a smoke flap near the top could be

木杆为他们的帐篷提供了圆锥形的基础，一些木杆能达到25英尺（7.6米）高。野牛的兽皮被缝合到了一起成为帐篷的墙体。用来建造帐篷的木杆和兽皮可以被迅速地取下来然后运到另一个地方。一旦部落确定了定居的场所，两三个人便可在不到两个小时的时间内建立起帐篷。

一个大家庭可以很舒适地住在一个圆锥形帐篷里，帐篷的直径有15英尺（4.57米），这么大的空间足够他们白天做饭晚上睡觉了。门，或者叫作开口，通常是朝向东方的，因为东边没有那么多的风。当在帐篷内做

hide *n.* 皮；毛皮
comfortably *adv.* 舒适地

stitch *v.* 缝
ciameter *n.* 直径

opened to let smoke escape, or closed to keep heat in the teepee during the long, cold winter months.

Not all Plains tribes lived in teepees. Village tribes—such as the Pawnee, Omaha, and Mandan—built more *permanent* shelters. These shelters were built long and low to the ground so that they could better withstand the strong winds that whipped across the *prairie*. Wood, bison skins, grass, and mud were combined to make homes and lodges. Large families lived and cooked in the lodge, and there was even enough room inside for a horse and the family's dogs.

饭的时候，靠近顶部的口盖可以卷起，以便散烟；当为帐篷供暖的时候，这个口盖又可以关闭，以便在漫长寒冷的冬季保持帐篷内的温度。

并不是所有的大平原部落都住在圆锥形帐篷里。村落部族——如波尼族，奥马哈族，还有曼丹族——建造了比圆锥形帐篷还要多的永久性居所。这些居所被建造得很长而且距离地面很低，这样的话能够更好地抵挡扫过大草原的强风。木材、野牛皮、草，还有泥被组合到了一起建造成他们的房屋。家族成员在棚屋里起居，棚屋里甚至为马和家狗留有足够的空间。

permanent *adj.* 永久的　　　　prairie *n.* （北美的）大草原

Making the Most of a Bison				
Hide *Clothes quivers dolls cradles bedding shields medicine bags rattles ropes saddles*			**Hair** *Headdresses ornaments medicine pillows rope balls*	
Tail *Brush whip*				**Horns** *cups* *powder horn* *spoons* *ladles* *toys* *ornaments*
Hoof *glue* *rattles*	**Meat** *food* *jerky*	**Bones** *tools* *weapons* *sled runners*		

充分利用野牛				
野牛皮 衣服、箭囊、玩偶、摇篮、寝具、盾、药物、袋子、拨浪鼓、绳子、鞍具			**野牛毛** 头饰、装饰物、药物、枕头、绳子、球	
野牛尾巴 刷子、鞭子				**野牛角** 杯子、药粉、号角、匙子、长柄勺、玩具、装饰物
野牛蹄 胶、拨浪鼓	**野牛肉** 食物、牛肉干	**野牛骨** 工具、武器、雪橇滑板		

quiver *n.* 箭囊
jerky *n.* 牛肉干

ornament *n.* 装饰物
ladle *n.* 长柄勺

Where Buffalo Once Roamed

Bison provided meat, shelter, and tools for many tribes in the Plains. Tribes found uses for all parts of the bison. Almost every part was eaten, including the organs. Bison skin was made into clothing, blankets, shoes, shields, and teepees. Their horns were made into spoons or *scoops*, or used as ornaments. Bison bones were used to make all kinds of tools, weapons, and everyday objects, including runners on children's sleds.

In the fall, bison gathered in huge herds— often of more than one million. Fall was the best time for hunting, and village tribes had

---

水牛栖息过的地方

北美野牛为生活在大平原上的许多部落提供了食物、住所和工具。这些部落发现了野牛身体各部分的用途。几乎每个部分都被吃掉，包括它们的器官。野牛皮被制成衣服、毯子、鞋子、住所，以及圆锥形帐篷。野牛角被制成匙子或勺子，或被当作装饰物使用。野牛骨被用来制造各种工具、武器和日常用品，包括孩子雪橇上的滑板。

秋天的时候，大群的北美野牛聚集到了一起——经常是百万以上的数量。秋季是狩猎的最佳时节，村落部族在这段时间进行一年一度的狩猎行

---

scoop *n.* 勺

their annual hunts at that time. Nomadic *tribes* would gather in larger groups, setting up camps and celebrating the *bounty* of the bison hunt.

Hunters rode out from camp on their horses until they found the bison herd. They would ride toward the herd until the bison started running. Then the hunters would ride right alongside the animals, spearing them or shooting them with either bows and arrows or guns. Bows were made of wood, with *bowstrings* made of bison tendons.

The hunters were able to shoot the bison with amazing accuracy while their horses were *galloping* full-speed through the herd.

动。游牧部落会结成更大的群体，他们建立起营地，庆祝猎取野牛所获得的战利品。

猎手骑着马从营地出发直至他们发现野牛群。他们会一直朝着野牛群骑行直至野牛开始奔跑。然后猎手会骑行在猎物旁边，用矛刺向它们，或者使用弓箭或枪支向它们射击。弓是木头制成的，而弓弦是由野牛腱制成的。

当他们所骑的马在野牛群中全速飞驰的时候，猎手能够以惊人的准确度射中野牛。有时一大群人会骑着马将野牛赶下悬崖，以致野牛跌落而亡。

tribe *n.* 部落
bowstring *n.* 弓弦

bounty *n.* 奖金；奖赏
gallop *ι.* （马）飞奔

Sometimes a large group of people riding horses would chase the bison off a cliff, so that the bison fell to their deaths.

When winter came, the bison would break up into smaller herds, and nomadic tribes broke up into smaller groups, too. Nomadic tribes followed the bison *migration* throughout the year while many tribes living in farming villages stayed in one place for the entire year. During the winter months, they lived off the big bison hunt and the crops they harvested.

Horses, Weapons, and Wars

Before Europeans brought horses to the United States in the 1500s, nomadic tribes moved and hunted on foot. Spanish *explorers*

冬季到来的时候，野牛会解散成小群，游牧部落也分成小群。游牧部落会一年四季跟随着野牛迁徙的足迹，而居住在农耕村落的部落却整年待在一个地方。在冬季，他们靠大狩猎获得的野牛和收割的庄稼生活。

马匹、武器、战争

在欧洲人于16世纪将马带到美国之前，游牧部落是通过步行来迁徙和狩猎的。西班牙的探险者将马引入了美国西南部，而后这些马开始奔跑

---

migration n. 迁徙

explorer n. 探险者

introduced horses in the southwest United States, and the horses quickly ran wild throughout the Plains.

Through trade (and stealing), more tribes began acquiring horses. By the 1700s, horses were fully a part of the Plains Native American lifestyle, and everything changed when people had the speed and power of these four-legged beasts. Members of the Plains tribes became excellent horsemen, and they rode horses into bison hunts and into wars.

Some of the Plains tribes had *reputations* as warring tribes. Most of the battles were small, often fought to steal horses from another tribe or to *avenge* a death. War was seen as a way to restore honor. As the U.S. Army and other Americans moved west, they posed a

---

在整个大平原上。

通过贸易（还有偷窃），越来越多的部落获得了马匹。到了18世纪，马匹已经完全成了大平原美洲原住民生活方式的一部分。当人们拥有了这些四脚兽的速度和力量时，一切都发生了改变。平原部落成员成了出色的骑手，他们以骑马的方式猎取野牛，也以这种方式进行战争。

作为交战部落，一些平原部落获得了名望。大部分战役的规模都很小，通常是为了从另一部落偷窃马匹或为一位死者报仇而进行的战斗。战争被看作是恢复荣誉的一种方式。当美国军队和其他美国人向西移动的时候，他们对大平原上部落的生活构成了威胁，这些部落为争取狩猎、耕

---

reputation *n.* 名望　　　　　　　　avenge *v.* 报（某事）之仇

threat to the *livelihood* of the Plains tribes, who fought for their right to hunt, farm the land, and preserve their traditions.

Celebration Ceremony

Members of the Plains tribes often gathered to sing, dance, and celebrate with friends. One important ceremony was the Summer Sun Dance. The Sun Dance was different from tribe to tribe, but all Sun Dance celebrations focused on thanking the Great Spirit for plentiful food. Because bison was an important food source, it was featured in Sun Dances.

A Sun Dance lasted for several days with *nonstop* dancing. Dancers also shook their heads and looked into the sun as long as

地、保护他们传统的权利而进行了斗争。

庆典仪式

平原部落成员经常聚到一起与朋友唱歌，跳舞，庆祝。其中一个重要的仪式就是夏季太阳舞。部落与部落之间的太阳舞是有区别的，但所有的太阳舞都以感谢为其带来丰富食物的大神为中心。因为北美野牛是其中一种重要的食物来源，因此该主题在太阳舞中得以突出体现。

太阳舞会一直不停地持续几天的时间。只要能够忍受，舞者会一直摇着头望着太阳，这会伤害他们的身体。他们希望在太阳舞结束的时候会看

livelihood *n.* 生计   nonstop *adj.* 不停的

their eyes could endure it, which could hurt them. They hoped they'd have a vision at the end of the Sun Dance and that *prosperity* would come to their tribe.

Even today, dances of celebration are important to many tribes. One of those dances is the Grass Dance (or Omaha Dance), which started around 1860 in the Omaha tribe, possibly as a warrior dance. Modern dancers wear *outfits* with lots of *fringe* and ribbon to look like the movement of prairie grass. Early dancers of the Grass Dance may have tied grass to their clothes. Some tribes used the Grass Dance to *flatten* the grass before larger tribal ceremonies, others used it to celebrate victory over an enemy. Now, the Grass Dance is performed in tribal competitions.

到美景，使他们的部落繁荣兴旺。

甚至在今日，庆祝舞蹈对很多部落来说仍然是非常重要的。其中的一种舞蹈叫作草舞（或奥马哈舞），这种舞蹈可能是作为一种勇士舞蹈在大约1860年起源于奥马哈部落。现代的舞者穿着带有许多穗子和带子的全套服装，跳起舞来看起来像草原上晃动的草一样。草舞的早期舞者会将草系到他们的衣服上。一些部落用跳草舞这种方式在更大的庆祝活动到来之前将草踏平，其他部落用这种方式庆祝对敌人赢得的一场胜利。如今，草舞用于部落间的比赛。

prosperity *n.* 繁荣；兴旺
fringe *n.* 穗；流苏

outfit *n.* 全套服装
flatten *v.* 把……弄平

Do You Know?

The sound of drums played a powerful role in celebrations and rituals. Many drums were handed down in a family from one generation to the next and were often named and blessed. Older drums were made of deer, elk, horse, or bison hides stretched over hollowed out sections of logs.

The Ghost Dance started among Lakota, or Sioux (sue), tribes who were forced onto *reservations* by the United States government. The Ghost Dance recalled days when there were millions of bison and food was *plentiful*. It also told of a hoped for time when all the settlers would be dead, and the Native Americans would have their land back. This dance scared the settlers who were moving into the Great Plains.

你知道吗？

　　鼓声在庆典仪式上起到了很大的作用。很多鼓在家庭中从一代传到了下一代，而且经常会被赋予名字并得到祝福。旧时的鼓是由鹿皮、麋鹿皮、马皮或野牛皮紧绷在圆木的空心部分制成的。

　　鬼魂舞来自于拉科塔族或苏族部落，他们被美国政府逼迫到了保留地。鬼魂舞是对当年拥有数以百万头野牛、食物富足的日子的回忆。它也讲述了他们盼望中的所有移民都死去，美洲原住民重新获得他们土地的那一刻时光。这个舞蹈让搬到大平原上的移民们感到恐惧。

reservation *n.* 保留地　　　　　　　plentiful *adj.* 充足的

Do You Know?

On December 29, 1890, U.S. Cavalry troops at Wounded Knee (in what is now South Dakota) were guarding a large group of Lakota people who had **surrendered**. *When the Lakota began performing the Ghost Dance, it* **provoked** *the soldiers and a bloody battle broke out. During the battle, two hundred Lakota were killed by the Army. The murdered Lakota—including men, women, and children—were buried in a mass grave. It was the last battle between the Army and tribal people.*

The Indian Wars

As settlers from the Eastern United States began moving onto the Plains to mine, farm, and build towns and railroads, they came into conflict with the Plains tribes. The Plains tribes and the settlers

你知道吗?

1890年12月29日，美国在伤膝河（现在的南达科塔州）的骑兵部队将已经投降的拉科塔族人民包围。当拉科塔人开始跳鬼魂舞时，激怒了美军士兵，一场血腥的战役爆发了。战役中，两百名拉科塔人被美军杀害。被杀害的拉科塔人——包括男人、妇女和儿童——被埋葬在了一起。这是美国军队与部落民族之间的最后一场战役。

印第安战争

随着美国东部殖民者开始向大平原迁移，进行采矿、耕种、修建城镇和铁路，他们与平原部落开始发生冲突。平原部落与殖民者为争夺土地发

surrender *v.* 包围　　　　provoke *v.* 激怒

fought over the land, and there was killing on both sides. Settlers demanded that the U.S. Army defend and protect them. The government sent troops to fight the Plains tribes, and those battles became known as "the Indian Wars".

The Plains tribes sometimes evenly matched the soldiers. The tribes knew the land well, and they used *guerrilla* , or secret warfare against the soldiers. But the U.S. Army *outnumbered* the tribes, and the army had more powerful guns than the tribes had.

However, the main reason that the Plains tribes eventually lost the wars was probably not the soldiers. By the time the U.S. Army reached many of the tribes, more than half the People had died from

---

生斗争，双方都有伤亡。殖民者要求美国军队保卫他们。政府派遣了部队与平原部落进行斗争，这些战役被人们称为"印第安战争"。

平原上的部落有时甚至能够敌得过美军士兵。这些部落对当地的地形非常熟悉，他们用游击战，或自己的诀窍与美军士兵进行战斗。但美军在数量上超过了这些部落，而且军队拥有比部落更具威力的枪炮。

然而，平原部落最终输掉战争最主要的原因可能与士兵无关。当美国军队抵达很多部落的时候，一多半的印第安人都死于疾病，如天花。殖民

---

guerrilla *n.* 游击战   outnumber *v.* （在数量上）压倒

diseases, such as *smallpox*. Settlers had brought diseases to the Plains—diseases that the Indians' bodies did not have *immunity*, or *resistance*.

The settlers and soldiers also killed most of the bison on the Plains, and without the bison, many tribes were left without the food and materials they needed to survive. The U.S. Cavalry used the method of running bison off a cliff to kill hundreds of thousands of bison at a time, leaving them to rot. In the late 1800s, most of the bison were gone.

Eventually, soldiers and settlers forced most of the Plains tribes onto reservations, or areas of land set aside for them. Often the

者将疾病带入了大平原——印第安人对这些疾病并没有免疫力或抵抗力。

殖民者和士兵也杀死了大部分生活在大平原上的野牛。没有了野牛，很多部落由于没有食物和维持生存的物资而被迫离开。美国骑兵用将野牛赶到悬崖的办法一次杀死了几十万的野牛，留下它们的尸体在那里腐烂。19世纪末，大部分的野牛都消失了。

最终，士兵和殖民者迫使平原部落到保留地或为他们留出的地区生活。通常，这些地区面积很小，而且是大平原上最贫瘠的耕地或狩猎地。

smallpox *n.* 天花   immunity *n.* 免疫力

resistance *n.* 抵抗力

444

areas were small and were the poorest farming or hunting land in the Great Plains.

Leaders

Leaders of the Lakota tribes resisted the U.S. government's efforts to put their people on reservations. Three of the most well known were Sitting Bull, Crazy Horse, and Red Cloud.

Sitting Bull was known as a *courageous* leader who fought to protect tribal lands. When gold was discovered in South Dakota in the mid-1870s, a rush of *prospectors* invaded tribal lands. In 1876, the U.S. government sent troops to protect the prospectors and ordered all Lakota to move to reservations. Sitting Bull refused. He called

---

领袖

拉科塔部落首领为美国政府试图将其子民赶到保留地这一行为进行了抵抗。最著名的三个首领分别是坐牛、疯马和红云。

坐牛被认为是一名勇敢的首领，他为保护部落土地而进行了英勇的斗争。19世纪70年代中期，殖民者在南达科塔发现了金子，大量的淘金者如潮水般涌入这片土地。1876年，美国政府派遣了军队来保护这些淘金者并命令所有拉科塔人搬到保留地。坐牛拒绝了这一命令。他将其他拉科

---

courageous *adj.* 勇敢的　　　　　　　　prospector *n.* 探矿者

together other Lakota as well as Arapaho and Cheyenne tribes, and they gathered at Little Bighorn Valley.

On June 25, 1876, George Armstrong Custer of the U.S. Army led his troops into the valley intending to *ambush* the Lakota, but Sitting Bull and his warriors were ready. The bloody battle ended with the death of Custer and his soldiers. The Battle of Little Bighorn is sometimes called "Custer's Last Stand".

Crazy Horse,who was known as Tashunca-uitco, was known as a *ferocious* warrior who fought to preserve the traditions of the Lakota. Crazy Horse stole his first horse before he was thirteen and led his first war party when he was still a teenager.

塔族人以及阿拉巴霍部落和夏安族部落召集到一起，并聚集在小巨角谷。

1876年6月25日，美国军队的乔治·阿姆斯特朗·卡斯特带领他的部队进入山谷，计划伏击拉科塔族人，但坐牛和他的勇士们早已做好准备。这场血腥的战役以卡斯特及其士兵的死亡而收场。小巨角战役有时被人们称为"卡斯特最后的阵地"。

疯马，也被称为Tashunca-uitco，是一位凶猛的勇士，他曾经为保护拉科塔族的传统而进行了战斗。疯马在他13岁之前偷来了他的第一匹马，当他还是个十几岁的青少年时就领导了第一支战斗部队。

ambush *v.* 伏击　　　　　　　　　　ferocious *adj.* 凶猛的

When the U.S. government ordered all Lakota bands onto reservations in 1876, Crazy Horse *resisted* and led other Lakota to resist, just as Sitting Bull did. After almost a year of battles, Crazy Horse saw that his people were struggling with the lack of bison too much to continue fighting. He was the last major chief to surrender.

Crazy Horse died in 1877. He did not allow any photographs to be taken of him, but his *likeness* is carved into the side of a mountain in South Dakota at the Crazy Horse Memorial.

Red Cloud, whose tribal name was Makhpiya-Luta was an important Lakota leader who led wars against tribes of Crows, Pawnees, Utes, and Shoshones. In 1866, Red Cloud began a

---

当美国政府在1876年命令所有拉科塔族人搬到保留地的时候，疯马进行了抵抗并带领其他拉科塔人进行抵抗，就像坐牛所做的一样。在经过近一年的战斗后，疯马发现他们严重缺乏野牛以至于不能继续战斗了。他是最后一个投降的首领。

疯马死于1877年。他不允许别人为他拍照片，但他的肖像却被雕刻在了南达科塔疯马纪念地的山上。

红云，部落名字为Makhpiya-Luta，是一位重要的拉科塔族首领。他领导了抵抗克劳族人、波尼族人、犹特族人和肖松尼族人的战争。为保护拉科塔族的土地不受进入到蒙大拿的淘金者侵略，1866年，红云开始了

---

resist *v.* 抵抗　　　　　　　　　　　　　likeness *n.* 肖像

series of attacks to protect Lakota land from miners traveling into Montana. To end the attacks, *the Fort Laramie Treaty*, which stated that the Lakota would abandon the *warpath* in exchange for money and goods, was signed. As part of the *treaty*, Red Cloud's Lakota band was supposed to stay only on reservation land. Although Red Cloud is said to have signed the treaty (marked with an "X"), there's little evidence that the terms of the treaty were fully explained to the Lakota leader.

The Plains Native Americans Today

Today, people from many Plains tribes come together to preserve their traditions. They hold tribal celebrations, practice speaking their native languages, and work to increase the number of bison.

一系列的攻击。为了结束攻击，双方签署了《拉勒米堡条约》，条约中规定拉科塔族人愿用金钱和商品交换，放弃敌对行动。作为条约的一部分，红云的拉科塔部落应只在保留地活动。尽管人们说是红云签署了这个条约（在这标上一个"×"），但几乎没有证据证明有人向这位拉科塔首领充分解释了条约中的条款。

当今大平原上的美洲原住民

现如今，很多平原部落的人们为保护他们的传统走到了一起。他们举行部落庆典，练习说自己的土著语言，致力于增加野牛的数量。

---

warpath *n.* 敌对行为   treaty *n.* 条约

Native Americans gather together across the country for *powwows*, which are a way to preserve their *heritage* through dance, music, arts, crafts, and food. Traditional dances have now become contests for prizes in addition to being done to celebrate a *bountiful* harvest or other occasion.

Many native languages, like the Lakota's, are disappearing because young people don't learn to speak or use them. Thirty years ago, many Lakota children in reservation schools spoke the same language as their grandmothers, grandfathers, and many generations of elders.

One problem with learning the Lakota language is not knowing how to pronounce some words. People working on The Lakota

---

全国各地的美洲原住民聚到一起举行印第安仪式，一种通过舞蹈、音乐、美术、手工艺和食物来保护他们文化遗产的一种方式。除了庆祝大丰收或其他场合，传统舞蹈现在已经成为大奖赛。

许多土著语言，如拉科塔语，正在消失，因为年轻人不去学说或使用它们。三十年前，保留地学校的很多拉科塔儿童说着与他们祖母、祖父以及上几代先辈们同样的语言。

学习拉科塔语言的一个问题是不知道如何发音。在印第安纳大学从事拉科塔语言项目的人们发明了一种计算机软件，通过这个软件，学生可以

---

powwow *n.* 帕瓦仪式　　　　　　　　　　　heritage *n.* 文化遗产
bountiful *adj.* 大量的

NATIVE AMERICANS OF THE GREAT PLAINS

Language Project at the University of Indiana created computer software that students can use to see and hear all the different ways a Lakota word might be pronounced. The program also shows ways a word might be used in different *communities*.

> *"We recognize the bison is a symbol of our strength and unity, and that as we bring our herds back to health, we will also bring our people back to health."*
>
> —*Fred DuBray,*
> *Cheyenne River Sioux*

To preserve another ancient tradition, more than forty tribes, including Lakota, Blackfoot, and Crow, came together to form the Intertribal Bison Cooperative. Some of the tribes were enemies

---

看见并听到拉科塔语发音的各种方式。这个软件也向学生展示了每个词汇用到不同团体中的方式。

> "我们承认野牛是我们力量和团结的象征，在使这群野牛恢复健康的同时，我们也将使我们的人民恢复健康"。
>
> ——弗雷德·杜布雷，夏安河苏族

为了保护另一古老的传统，四十多个部落，包括拉科塔族，黑脚部落以及克劳族，团结到一起建立了跨部落美洲野牛合作社。虽然一些部落在

---

community *n.* 团体

23 MCGRAW-HILL

hundreds of years ago, but now they are united in their efforts to bring bison back to the Great Plains. The bison reminds today's tribes of how their *ancestors* lived in harmony with nature, the animals also also represent the spirit many tribes are trying to preserve. More than 8,000 bison have been *reintroduced* to tribal lands through the Inter Tribal Bison Cooperative's efforts.

几百年前互为敌人，但现在他们团结一致为将野牛重新带回大平原而共同努力。野牛使当今的部落想起他们的祖先如何与大自然和谐共处，它们也代表了很多部落想要努力保护野牛的一种精神。在跨部落美洲野牛合作社的努力下，八千多头野牛重新返回了大平原。

ancestor *n.* 祖宗；祖先   reintroduce *v.* 重新引入

02

Ancient Cliff Dwellers

The Four Corners

Mesa Verde National Park, founded in 1906, is the first national park in the United States established to honor human *accomplishments*. Located where the states of Utah, Colorado, Arizona, and New Mexico meet, the park contains many *cliff dwellings* that are among the most striking examples of early human *architecture* in North America. The builders used great skill,

古代悬崖居民

四角地

梅萨维德国家公园建于1906年，是美国为向人类成就致敬而建立的第一座国家公园。公园位于犹他州、科罗拉多州、亚利桑那州和新墨西哥州的交会处，这里有许多悬崖屋，是北美早期人类建筑中最引人注目的典型建筑之一。建造者利用精湛的工艺，在没有现代工具和机器的情况下建成了这些非同寻常的居所。

accomplishment *n.* 成就
dwelling *n* 住所

cliff *n.* 悬崖
architecture *n.* 建筑物

creating these unusual dwellings without the aid of modern tools or machines.

Who lived in these structures, and how did they live? Why did they make their homes in the cliffs? Why did they leave, and where did they go? These are some of the questions we will explore.

> **Do You Know?**
>
> *Mesa Verde National Park is located in the Four Corners area, the only place in the United States where the corners of four states meet. The marker indicating the point is a tourist attraction.*

Evidence

The early people who lived in the Four Corners area are called *prehistoric* people, because they left no written records. We know

是谁住在这些建筑物里？他们又是如何生活的呢？为什么他们在悬崖上修建家园？他们为什么又离开那里，他们又要往哪里去呢？这些都是我们要探索的问题。

> **你知道吗？**
>
> 梅萨维德国家公园位于四角地地区，这里是美国唯一一处四个州交会的地方。显示交会点的这个标志物是一处观光胜地。

证据

居住在四角地的早期居民被称作史前人，因为他们没有留下文字记

prehistoric *adj.* 史前的

about them because we've found many remains of their culture buried in the ground.

Mesa Verde is located in a high, flat desert surrounded by mountains. The arid, or dry, conditions at Mesa Verde are ideal for preserving *skeletons*, *mummies*, dwellings, tools, and trash piles. These remains have helped *archaeologists* to study the lives of the early people who lived in the area. Other remains include pictographs, or paintings on stone, and *petroglyphs*, or pictures carved in stone.

Paleo-Indians

To understand the story of the cliff dwellers, we need to go back in time. Scientists believe that at least 14,000 years ago, during the

---

录。我们之所以知道他们是因为我们发现了很多埋于地下的文化遗址。

梅萨维德位于被高山环抱的平坦沙漠。这里干旱（或干燥）的条件适合保存骨骼、木乃伊、悬崖屋、工具及其废弃物。这些遗迹帮助了考古学家对生活在这片区域的早期人类进行研究。其他遗迹包括史前石壁画（或叫作石头上的绘画）和岩石画（或叫作雕刻在石头上的图画）。

古印第安人

要想了解悬崖居民的故事，我们需要将时光倒流。科学家相信，至

---

skeleton *n.* 骨骼
archaeologist *n.* 考古学家

mummy *n.* 木乃伊
petroglyph *n.* （史前的）岩画

Ice Age, ancient people crossed a land bridge from northern Russia to Alaska in North America. Hundreds of years later, some of their *descendants* traveled far enough south to reach the Four Corners area.

The first Four Corners people were called Paleo-Indians, and they survived by hunting and gathering. Men used large spears to hunt huge herd animals, including elephant-like animals called *mammoths* and *mastodons*, and giant bison. Women gathered nuts, berries, and other wild plants. The Paleo-Indians did not have permanent homes. Instead, they moved from place to place following the animals they hunted. They camped in caves or built simple shelters.

少14,000年前，在冰河世纪，古人穿过了北俄罗斯至北美阿拉斯加的大陆桥。几百年后，他们后代中的一些人向南旅行到达了四角地。

人们称这些首先到达四角地的人为"古印第安人"，他们靠狩猎和采集为生。男人使用大型矛猎取野兽，包括与大象外形类似叫作猛犸象和乳齿象的动物和巨型野牛。妇女采集坚果，浆果和其他野生植物。古印第安人没有固定的居所。相反，他们跟随着所要猎取的动物足迹从一个地方迁徙到另一个地方。他们在洞穴里宿营，或者建造简易的居所。

---

descendant *n.* 后代
mastodon *n.* 乳齿象

mammoth *n.* 猛犸象

Archaic People

When the Ice Age ended about 10,000 years ago, temperatures became warmer, causing the *extinction* of many large animals and turning large grasslands into deserts. The Four Corners people had to adapt to these changes and find new ways to survive. Archaeologists call these people the *Archaic* people.

Like their Paleo-Indian *ancestors*, the Archaic people were hunters and gatherers. But the animals they hunted were smaller and provided less meat than the ones their ancestors hunted. The Archaic people began to rely more on plants for food.

The Archaic people made different tools from those of the Paleo-Indians—smaller spear points for hunting deer and bighorn sheep,

古代人

冰河世纪在大约10,000年前结束，天气在这个时候开始变暖，导致了很多大型动物的灭绝，大草原变成了沙漠。四角地居民不得不适应这些变化并找到新的生存方式。考古学家将这些人称为古代人。

像他们的古印第安人祖先一样，古代人也是猎手和采集者。但他们猎取的动物要小很多，因此不能像他们祖先猎取的动物那样提供那么多的肉。古代人开始更多地依赖植物来获取食物。

古代人制作的工具与古印第安人有所不同——他们用更小的矛型刀尖

extinction *n.* 灭绝
ancestor *n.* 祖先

archaic *adj.* 古代的

and nets and traps for catching rabbits and birds. Women used special tools for chopping and *grinding* roots, seeds, nuts, and wild plants.

Early Tools

The first grinding stones and bowls were made during the Archaic people's time. Similar tools are still used by their descendants in the Southwest.

Ancient Puebloans

By about 2,000 years ago, life in the Four Corners had changed in important ways. People had learned to grow their own food instead of relying on wild animals and wild plants. Agriculture changed their way of life. These people were called the Ancient Puebloans.

猎取鹿和大角羊，用网和陷阱捕捉兔子和鸟。妇女使用特殊的工具削磨根茎、种子、坚果和野生植物。

早期工具

第一个磨石和磨碗是在古代人时期出现的。分布在西南部的后代使用着类似的工具。

古普韦布洛人

到了大约2,000年前，四角地人的生活方式发生了重大改变。人们学会了自己种植食物，而不是单纯依赖野生动物和植物。农业改变了他们的生活方式。这段时期的人被叫作古普韦布洛人。

---

grind *v.* 磨

The earliest Ancient Puebloans still relied mostly on hunting and gathering. However, growing their own food, such as corn and *squash*, on the open flat land allowed them to feed a larger group of people. It also gave them a source of food they could depend on.

Making Baskets

As the Ancient Puebloans grew more food, they found ways to store it. Women began to use plant fibers and tree bark to make baskets. Some baskets held food, while others were woven so tightly that they could hold water. Because baskets could not be placed over a fire, women cooked by placing hot rocks into baskets filled with water. The women also began making *sandals* from plant fibers.

最早的古普韦布洛人仍主要依靠狩猎和采集为生。然而，在宽阔平坦的土地上种植他们自己的食物，如玉米和南瓜属植物，让他们能够供养更多的人。这也给予了他们可以依靠的食物来源。

编篮子

随着古普韦布洛人种植越来越多的食物，他们找到了储存食物的方法。妇女开始使用植物纤维和树皮编篮子。一些篮子用来装食物，另一些篮子编织得严密到能够装水。由于篮子不能放到火上，妇女通过将热的岩石放到装着水的篮子里进行烹饪。她们也开始用植物纤维制作凉鞋。

---

squash *n.* 南瓜小果   sandal *n.* 凉鞋

As the Ancient Puebloans grew more crops and made more tools and baskets, they moved around less. Even as agriculture became more important to the Ancient Puebloan way of life, men continued to hunt using spears and nets. During this time, they lived in caves along cliffs and *canyon* walls.

Over time, the Ancient Puebloans relied more on agriculture to feed their growing population. By about 1,500 years ago, they grew beans in addition to corn and squash. Having a reliable food source from farming allowed them to stay in one place.

They built *temporary* houses, called pit houses, near their fields. These houses were built on top of shallow pits dug in the ground.

随着古普韦布洛人种植越来越多的庄稼并生产出更多的工具和篮子，他们迁徙得不那么频繁了。即使农业对古普韦布洛人的生活方式变得更加重要，但男人仍继续使用矛和网进行狩猎活动。在这段时期，他们住在沿着悬崖和峡谷峭壁的洞穴里。

随着时间的推移，古普韦布洛人越来越多地依赖农业以供养其不断增加的人口。到了大约1,500年前，除了玉米和南瓜属植物，他们开始种植豆子。通过耕种获得了可靠的食物来源让他们能够在固定的地方生活。

他们在田地附近搭建叫作洞穴房的临时房屋。这些房屋搭建在从地下挖出的浅坑上面。侧面和顶部由树枝、树皮和泥土建成。考古学家相信古

---

canyon *n.* 峡谷   temporary *adj.* 临时的

The sides and ceilings were constructed of tree branches, bark, and soil. Archaeologists believe the Ancient Puebloans were a peaceful people because no weapons of war have been found. Also, the location of their houses suggests that they did not feel *threatened* by enemies since houses built in the open are hard to defend.

Another important change during this time was the production of *pottery*. Tribes from Mexico taught the Ancient Puebloans pottery making. Although women continued to make baskets, using clay pots allowed them to cook over an open fire. Clay pots also stored food better.

Men started using bows and arrows during this time, which was

普韦布洛人是爱好和平的人，因为没有发现任何战争的迹象。此外，他们建造房屋的地点也说明了他们并未感受到来自敌人的威胁，因为在野外所建造的房屋很难防卫。

这段时期另一个重要的变化是陶器的发明。来自于墨西哥的部落教会了古普韦布洛人陶器制造术。尽管妇女仍继续编篮子，但使用黏土锅能够让她们直接在明火上烹饪。黏土锅也能够更好地存储食物。

这段时期，男人开始使用弓箭，这要比用矛狩猎更加容易，成功的几

threaten *v.* 威胁；恐吓　　　　　pottery *n.* 陶器（尤指手工制）

easier and more successful than spear hunting. These changes allowed the population to continue growing as food became more plentiful.

The Ancient Puebloans also used animal hair *twisted* with cotton string to make warm socks and leg coverings. Sometimes they also wove feathers and string made from *yucca* plants to make clothing.

Do You Know?

Chaco Canyon, in northwestern New Mexico, was an important cultural center made up of 12 large pueblos. The largest, Pueblo Bonito, housed about 1,000 people. Archaeologists believe that Chaco Canyon was a trade center for surrounding communities.

率也变得更大。随着食物更加富足，这些变化使得人口持续增长。

古普韦布洛人也将动物毛与棉绳捻到一起制成温暖的袜子和腿套。有时他们也将羽毛和丝兰制成的线编织在一起做衣服。

你知道吗？

位于新墨西哥州西北部的查科大峡谷是由12个大普韦布洛组成的重要文化中心。最大的一个是普韦布洛博尼托镇，这里住着约1,000人。考古学家相信查科大峡谷是周边群落的贸易中心。

---

twist *v.* 捻；搓　　　　　　yucca *n.* 丝兰（叶剑形坚挺，常种于室内）

Building Larger Houses

Around 1,300 years ago, the population had grown so much that the Ancient Puebloans were living in larger groups. They built *rectangular* houses completely above ground. They used tree *limbs* and bark for a frame, then covered the wood with adobe (soil containing clay). Over time, they started building houses with sandstone blocks stacked and held together with adobe. The houses were built side by side, creating large buildings called pueblos. Pueblo is a Spanish word that means town or village. The Ancient Puebloans also built underground circular structures called kivas, which were used for holding ceremonies.

The Ancient Puebloan culture thrived for several hundred years.

建造大房子

大约1,300年前，古普韦布洛人口激增，因此他们以更大的群落共同生活。他们完全在地上建造长方形的房子。他们使用树枝和树皮建造框架，然后土坯（含有黏土的土壤）将木材覆盖。慢慢地，他们开始用砂岩块建造房屋，他们把砂岩块堆叠到一起，然后用土坯将其粘到一起。这些并排建造的房屋就是叫作普韦布洛的大型建筑。普韦布洛是西班牙语，意思是城镇或村庄。古普韦布洛人也建造了叫作大地穴的地下圆形建筑，这种建筑用来举行仪式。

古普韦布洛文化繁荣了几百年。人们开发出了帮助其庄稼生长的新方

rectangular *adj.* 长方形的   limb *n.* 树枝

The people developed new ways to help their crops grow. They built dams, *reservoirs*, and *terraces* to manage water for their fields. Successful crops allowed them to feed their growing population.

The types of pottery they made changed. Women made everyday pottery that was used for cooking and storing food. Everyday pottery was gray with a rough outer texture that helped heat the food inside. They also made pottery that was rubbed and *polished* to create a smooth surface for decoration or trade. They decorated this pottery with complex, colorful designs using paint made from wild plants.

Moving to the Cliffs

Around 900 years ago, the Ancient Puebloans moved from

法。他们建造大坝、水库和梯田对农田灌溉进行管理。风调雨顺让他们能够供养不断增加的人口。

他们制造陶器的方式也发生了改变。妇女制造用来做饭和存放食物的日常陶器。这些灰色的日常陶器外表质地粗糙，这样有助于对陶器内的食物进行加热。她们也制造经过打磨的陶器，这些表面光滑的陶器可以进行装饰或买卖。她们使用由野生植物制成的颜料，用色彩鲜艳复杂的图案对陶器进行装饰。

搬到悬崖峭壁上去

大约900年前，古普韦布洛人从开阔的田野迁徙到有防护的悬崖壁架

---

reservoir *n.* 水库　　　　　terrace *n.* 梯田
polish *v.* 擦亮；磨光

open land to protected ledges on cliffs and canyon walls. The cliff dwellings found at Mesa Verde and other places in the Four Corners area are typical of this time period. These houses were up to five stories tall, providing housing for hundreds of people. The cliff dwellers used ladders and ropes to get to their homes. They also cut finger and toe holds into the rocks for climbing up the walls.

About 600 cliff dwellings are located in Mesa Verde National Park. Cliff Palace, the largest, had 217 rooms and 23 *kivas*. The smallest rooms may have been storage rooms rather than living *quarters*.

和峡谷峭壁上。在四角地梅萨维德和其他地方发现的悬崖屋是这段时期具有代表性的建筑。这些建筑有五层楼高，为数以百计的人提供住房。悬崖居民使用梯子和绳索返回家中。他们也在岩石上切割指孔以便能够沿着峭壁向上爬。

在梅萨维德国家公园大约有600个悬崖屋。绝壁宫殿是最大的一个，它拥有217间房屋和23个大地穴。最小的房间可能是存储间而不是住处。

kiva *n.* 大地穴   quarter *n.* 住处；住房

A Safety Issue?

Some archaeologists believe the Ancient Puebloans were being attacked by other tribes and needed homes they could easily defend. Many cliff dwellings could only be reached with ladders. The people in them could pull their ladders inside, leaving their enemies no way to enter. Although this idea makes sense, there is little evidence *that this was the reason for the move.*

Archaeologists were puzzled by the Ancient Puebloans' move from open areas to cliff dwellings. They believe that as the Ancient Puebloan population grew, more farmland was needed. Moving to

安全问题？

一些考古学家认为古普韦布洛人是因为受到了其他部落的攻击而需要一个可以容易防守的家园。许多悬崖屋只能用梯子才能到达。住在那里的人们可以将梯子拉进屋内，使敌人无法进入。尽管这个想法讲得通，但认为这就是他们迁徙的原因还缺乏证据。

考古学家一直困惑于古普韦布洛人从开阔地迁移到悬崖屋这一举动。他们认为随着古普韦布洛人口的增加，他们应该需要更多的农田。搬到悬崖屋让他们放弃了更多适合耕种的土地。而且古普韦布洛人也可能需要开

evidence *n.* 证据

cliff dwellings freed more flat land for growing crops. The Ancient Puebloans also may have needed to create new fields to replace old fields that were *overused* and had lost the ability to grow food well.

Another possible reason for the move might have been for warmth during winter. The weather was getting colder during this time. Most cliff dwellings face south or southwest, where the sun's rays could warm the rock walls of their homes.

Building Dwellings

Building the cliff dwellings was a huge challenge for the Ancient Puebloans, who lacked machines and used only stone tools. They were skilled at designing structures that made the best use of the

---

发新的田地来取代已经过度使用的旧农田，因为旧农田已经失去种植食物的能力。

迁徙的另一个可能因素或许是由于冬季的温度。这段时期，气候开始变冷。大部分的悬崖屋都是朝南或西南，阳光可以从这个方向照射到岩壁上使他们的家变得温暖。

建造居所

建造悬崖屋对于缺乏机器、仅使用石器工具的古普韦布洛人来说是一个巨大的挑战。精通于设计出充分利用空间的建筑物。建造者用削成形的

---

overuse *v.* 过度使用

space. The builders made walls from large stones chipped into shape and held together with *adobe*. They covered the walls with adobe, sometimes painting designs on the insides of the walls.

Builders made upper floors by laying large wooden poles across the tops of walls and placing smaller poles across the *beams*. Next a layer of sticks or bark was piled on. Then they added a thick layer of adobe to hold it together.

Daily Life

The Ancient Puebloans probably spent most of their time outside working together in groups. Women cooked, ground corn, carried water, and made pottery and baskets. Men wove cloth, farmed

---

巨石建造墙体，用土坯将这些巨石结合到一起。他们用土坯将墙体覆盖，有时会在内墙上涂上图案。

建造者将大木杆横跨放到墙的顶部，将小一些的木杆横跨到梁上，这样就建成了上层楼面。接下来再叠放一层木棍或树皮，然后添加一层厚厚的土坯以使其结合到一起。

日常生活

古普韦布洛人可能将他们大部分的时间用于集体户外工作。妇女做饭、研磨玉米、挑水、制作陶器和篮子。男人编织布料、耕地、狩猎、用

---

adobe *n.* 土坯

beam *n.* 梁；横梁

crops, hunted, and made tools out of stone, wood, and plant *fibers*. Children worked alongside their parents, learning adult roles by watching and practicing. They also took care of turkeys and spent time at play. During the winter some work was done inside the dwellings. Archaeologists believe that rooms were used year-round for sleeping.

Trade with other tribes was an important aspect of Ancient Puebloan life. The map below shows some of the items they traded.

石头、木材和植物纤维制造工具。孩子们在父母周围，通过观看和练习来学习成年人的规则。他们也照看火鸡，玩耍。冬季，一些工作在屋内完成。考古学家认为屋子一年四季都是用来睡觉的。

与其他部落进行贸易是古普韦布洛人生活的一个重要方面。下面的图表显示了他们贸易的部分物品。

---

fiber *n.* 纤维

Mesa Verde Trading	
Turquoise	*Furs*
Shells	*Pottery*
Salt	*Corn*
Cotton	*Beads*

Spiritual Life

Because modern kivas are still used by the descendants of the Ancient Puebloans, we know they were used for *religious* ceremonies.

梅萨维德的贸易	
绿松石	毛皮
贝　壳	陶器
盐	玉米
棉　花	珠子

精神生活

因为现在的大地穴仍为古普韦布洛人的后代所用，因此我们知道这些大地穴是用来进行宗教仪式的。这些大地穴也可能被用作家庭聚会，在冬

religious *adj.* 宗教的

They were probably also used for family gatherings, as guest rooms, and as workspaces in winter.

People entered kivas with ladders. Each kiva had a fire pit in the center and a shaft providing fresh air. Half of the Mesa Verde kivas also had a small hole in the floor called a sipapu. The hole represented a *doorway* between the spirit world and the real world. Archaeologists think that the Ancient Puebloans, like their modern descendants, believed that all living things have both a spirit self and a physical self. They also believed in life after death.

Leaving the Cliffs

Between 1280 and 1295, the Ancient Puebloans left the cliff

季当作客房以及工作场所。

人们用梯子进入大地穴。每个大地穴的中心都有一个燃池，还有一个提供新鲜空气的天井。梅萨维德一半的大地穴地面上也有一个小洞，这个小洞叫作斯帕普。这个小洞代表着精神世界与现实世界之间的出入口。考古学家认为古普韦布洛人与他们的后代一样，他们都相信所有的生物都有精神自我和身体自我，他们也相信死后还能重生。

告别悬崖

1280至1295年间，古普韦布洛人离开了悬崖屋向南迁移到了新墨西

doorway *n.* 门口

dwellings and moved south to New Mexico and Arizona. No one knows for sure why they moved, but archaeologists believe that the climate kept changing and that this played an important role. It got colder, causing a shorter growing season for crops. Watering crops became harder because there were long periods of time with little or no rain. In addition, the soil may have been so overused that growing enough food for the large *population* became impossible.

Perhaps by the time the Ancient Puebloans left Mesa Verde, they had cut down most of the trees for *firewood* and for building pueblos. Hunters may have killed so many wild animals that the meat supply was gone.

哥州和亚利桑那州。没有人知道他们迁移的确切原因，但考古学家认为气候的不断变化，起到了重要作用。天气变冷，导致了庄稼的生长期变短。由于长时间没有降水，因此灌溉庄稼就变得更加困难。除此之外，土地被严重地过度利用，不能为庞大的人口种植足够的食物。

或许古普韦布洛人离开梅萨维德的时候，他们已经砍伐掉了大部分的树木当作木柴以及建造普韦布洛。猎手可能猎杀了过多的野生动物，以致他们用尽了肉食供给。

population *n.* 人口　　　　　　　　firewood *n.* 木柴

Some people think that enemy tribes drove out the cliff dwellers. However, that is unlikely, because there are no remains of other cultures at Mesa Verde after the Ancient Puebloans left. Archaeologists find older remains deeper in the ground and newer remains closer to the ***surface***. If enemies drove out the cliff dwellers, evidence of their culture would be found on top of the Ancient Puebloan remains.

Modern-Day Descendants

When the ancient cliff dwellers left Mesa Verde, some moved

有人认为是敌对部落赶走了悬崖居民。然而，这不大可能，因为自古普韦布洛人离开后，在梅萨维德没有其他文化的遗迹。考古学家在地下更深处发现了更早的遗迹，在接近地表处发现了更晚的遗迹。如果是敌人赶走了悬崖居民，在古普韦布洛遗迹的上面应该能找到他们文化的证据。

后裔现今的状况

当古代悬崖居民离开梅萨维德的时候，一些人迁移到了南方，沿着

---

surface *n.* 表层

south, settling along the Rio Grande River in New Mexico. These are the ancestors of the modern Pueblo tribes. Others moved to Arizona, eventually forming the Zuni and Hopi tribes.

Modern tribes have continued many of the traditions of the ancient cliff dwellers. The Pueblo, Zuni, and Hopi peoples continue to farm, conduct ceremonies, and perform *rituals*. They still honor their *connection* with the land and the spirit world. They are among the finest artists in the world, creating *exquisite* pottery, jewelry, baskets, carvings, and weavings.

新墨西哥州的里奥格兰德河定居下来。这些人就是当代普韦布洛部族的祖先。其他人迁移到了亚利桑那州，最终形成了祖尼部落和霍皮部落。

当代部落继承了古代悬崖居民的很多传统。普韦布洛人，祖尼人还有霍皮人依然耕种、进行典礼、举行仪式。他们仍然认为现实世界与精神世界存在联系。他们是世界上最好的艺术家，为人类创造出了精致的陶器、首饰、篮子、雕刻和编织品。

---

ritual *n.* 仪式；礼节　　　　　　　　　　　connection *n.* 联系
exquisite *adj.* 精致的

Preserving the Past Corners

*We must protect historic artifacts of ancient people. Follow these rules to preserve ruins and **artifacts**.*

1. *Look, but don't touch. It is against the law to keep artifacts.*

2. *Do not touch or draw on walls, petroglyphs, or pictographs.*

3. *Do not climb on walls. Many walls are **fragile** and easily damaged.*

Protecting the Cliff Dwellings

In the late 1800s many people visited the cliff dwellings—some

保护历史

我们必须保护古人留下的具有历史意义的手工艺品。按照下面的原则保护遗迹和手工艺品。

1.看，但不要碰。持有古代手工艺品是非法的。

2.不要接触墙壁，岩石画或石壁画，也不要在上面乱画。

3.不要攀爬墙壁。很多墙壁是易碎的，很容易破坏。

保护悬崖屋

19世纪末，很多人来到了悬崖屋进行参观——有些人在现场拍照、

artifact *n.* 手工艺品　　　　　fragile *adj.* 易碎的

photographed, drew, and described the sites, but others took artifacts from the dwellings to sell. Over time, people became concerned about protecting the cliff dwellings from damage and *looting*. The concern led to the creation of Mesa Verde National Park in 1906. The National Park Service protects the cliff dwellings, as well as allowing visitors to enjoy them. *Educational* exhibits at Mesa Verde and other sites in the Southwest teach people about the Ancient Puebloan way of life.

画画、描述，但另一些人却带走了悬崖屋的手工艺品进行贩卖。随着时间的流逝，人们开始关注保护悬崖屋不受破坏和洗劫。人们对悬崖屋的关注使梅萨维德国家公园于1906年得以建立。国家公园管理局对悬崖屋加以保护并允许游客进行参观。在梅萨维德和西南部其他地方进行的教育展览让人们了解古普韦布洛人的生活方式。

---

looting n. 抢劫；劫掠   educational adj. 教育的

03

Desert People

Demanding Deserts

Imagine that you are standing alone in the desert. There is total silence, except for the soft call of a *dove*. The fresh breeze feels good on your face. The sun begins to rise over the mountains, which slowly change from black to light purple. Then the sun's *rays* peek out and turn the morning into day.

Look around you. Imagine that your family and friends also live here. What would your lives be like? A few hundred years ago, there

---

荒漠人

苛刻的沙漠

想象一下你独自一人站在沙漠里的情景。除了鸽子轻柔的呼唤，这里寂静无声。清风吹拂到你的脸上，那种感觉舒服极了。太阳爬上了山岗，群山在晨光的衬托下逐渐地从黑色变成了淡紫色。阳光直射了过来，天亮了。

看看你的周围。想象一下你的家人还有朋友也住在这里。你们的生活会是什么样的呢？几百年前，在这片沙漠里，没有汽车，没有自行车，也

---

dove *n.* 鸽子

ray *n.* 光线；光束

were no cars, no bicycles, and no paved roads in this desert. How would you travel from place to place?

Imagine that you feel hungry in this desert. There are no stores or supermarkets. Can you feel the thirst in the back of your throat? Where would you find water to drink? You look around. There are no *drinking fountains* and no flowing rivers. There is not a single cloud in the light blue sky.

What Exactly Is a Desert?

Would you know a desert if you saw one? Would there be camels walking on sand dunes? Would there be *rattlesnakes*, *saguaro* cacti, and tall mountains? Or would the land be rocky, with only a few *shrubs* and trees?

没有铺有路面的道路。你会怎样从一个地方旅行到另一个地方呢？

再想象一下在这片沙漠里当你感觉到饥饿时的情景吧。这里没有商店，也没有超市。你能感觉到喉底干渴的那种感觉吗？在哪儿能找到水喝？看看周围，这里没有自动饮水机，也没有流淌的河流。淡蓝色的天空中没有一片云彩。

沙漠到底是什么？

如果你曾经看到过沙漠，你会认识它吗？那里会有骆驼行走在沙丘上吗？那里有没有响尾蛇、仙人掌和高山？除了少量的灌木丛和树木，地面上是否有很多岩石？

---

drinking fountain 喷泉式饮水器　　　　　　　rattlesnake　*n.*　响尾蛇
saguaro　*n.*　树形仙人掌　　　　　　　　　　shrub　*n.*　灌木丛

All three of these descriptions are deserts. Many types of deserts exist. Deserts may have rocky mountains, *graveled* plateaus, or rolling sand dunes. Some desert areas even have streams and rivers.

Scientists disagree on the exact definition of the word "desert". But they do agree that deserts share some common traits. Compared with the rest of the world, deserts are dry places. They usually receive less than 25.4 centimeters (10 in.) of *precipitation* a year. Deserts tend to have dry soil and not much vegetation. Although some deserts can get pretty cold, most deserts are sunny and hot.

　　上面所描写的就是沙漠。沙漠的类型有很多。沙漠可能会有由岩石构成的山脉、充满沙砾的高原，或者起伏的沙丘。一些沙漠地区甚至有小溪和河流。

　　科学家对"沙漠"一词的准确定义持有不同的看法。但他们同意沙漠所表现出的一些共同的特性。与世界其他地方相比，沙漠是比较干燥的地方。沙漠通常每年有不到25.4厘米（10英寸）的降水。沙漠的土地往往是干旱的，而且植被也不多。尽管有些沙漠会变得非常寒冷，但大部分沙漠都是晴朗炎热的。

---

graveled　*adj.*　（道路等）砾石铺的　　　　　　　　precipitation　*n.*　降水

> *Desert: a dry, barren area of land, especially one covered with sand, that is* **characteristically desolate**, *waterless, and without* **vegetation**.
>
> *This is the official New Oxford American* **definition** *of desert.*

Desert Survival

So if deserts are such hot and dry places, how have people survived? Where did they find food to eat and water to drink? What did they use to build their homes?

For thousands of years, desert people have found answers to these questions. They have used local resources for food, water,

---

> 沙漠：一片干燥、贫瘠的土地，尤其是被沙子覆盖，它的特点是荒凉、无水、没有植被。
>
> 这是《新牛津美语大辞典》中对"沙漠"一词的正式定义。

沙漠求生

那么既然沙漠是如此干燥炎热的地方，那里的人们如何生存呢？他们到哪里去找吃的食物和喝的水？他们用什么建造房屋？

几千年的时间里，沙漠中的人们已经找到了问题的答案。他们的衣、食、住都来自于当地的资源。沙漠中的人们找到了适应的方式。每一片沙

---

characteristically *adv.* 有代表性地
vegetation *n.* 植被

desolate *adj.* 荒凉的
definition *n.* 定义

and shelter. Desert people have found ways to *adapt*. Each desert is different. And each desert has its own answers.

In this book, you will learn about two interesting groups of desert people: the Tohono O'odham and the Bedouin. You will also read about sand dunes, wild foods, villages, hunting, and more. You will even read about dogs that ride on camels!

World Deserts Comparison Table				
	Sonoran	*Sahara*	*Gobi*	*Atacama*
Climate	*Good rainfall for a desert*	*Very hot and very dry*	*Cold and windy*	*Driest desert in the world*

漠都是不同的，因此每一片沙漠都有它自己的答案。

这本书中，你将了解到两个有意思的荒漠人部族：托何那奥丹部族和贝都因人。你还将通过阅读了解到沙丘、野味、村庄、狩猎以及更多的内容。你甚至能够通过阅读而知道有一种骑在骆驼上的狗！

世界沙漠对照表				
	索诺兰沙漠	撒哈拉沙漠	戈壁沙漠	阿塔卡玛沙漠
气候	降水充足	非常炎热干燥	寒冷多风	世界上最干燥的沙漠

adapt *v.* 适应

Continent	North America	Africa	Asia	South America
Size (sq. km.)	310,800	9,064,960	1,036,000	139,860
Terrain	*Flat* basins, mountains	Gravel plains, mountains, sand dunes	Stony, sandy soil, grasslands	Sand, salt basins, *lava*
Example of desert people	Tohono O'odham	Bedouin	Mongols	Atacama Indians
Compare these four deserts. Notice that they are all very different.				

所处大陆	北美洲	非洲	亚洲	南美洲
面积（平方公里）	310,800	9064,960	1,036,000	139,860
地形	平坦的盆地、山地	布满砾石的平原、山地、沙丘	多石、沙质土壤、草原	沙地、含盐盆地、火山熔岩
生活的部族	托何那奥丹部族	贝都因人	蒙古人	阿塔卡玛印第安人
比较一下这四个沙漠。注意它们都大不相同。				

flat *adj.* 平坦的

lava *n.* 火山熔岩

The Tohono O'odham

Tohono O'odham means "The Desert People". The Tohono O'odham are Native Americans who still live in the Sonoran Desert.

For years, they have watched the sun rise over Baboquivari, their *sacred* mountain. They believe that Baboquivari is where "Elder Brother" created them from the clay of the earth. "Elder Brother" gave the desert to the O'odham and taught them how to use its plants.

The O'odham lived in villages. They slept in round homes with flat roofs. These homes were made of dried mud, branches, and grass. There was one main room with a fire pit in the middle. Families slept

---

托何那奥丹部族

托何那奥丹的意思是"沙漠人"。托何那奥丹人是现在仍然生活在索诺兰沙漠中的美洲原住民。

多年来,他们习惯于注视着太阳爬上他们的圣山——巴布奇瓦里山。他们相信巴布奇瓦里山是"老大哥"从泥土中将他们创造出来的地方。"老大哥"将这片沙漠送给了奥丹人并教会他们如何使用这里的作物。

奥丹人居住在村庄里。他们睡在带有平屋顶的圆形房屋里。这些房屋是由干泥浆、树枝和草建成的。屋子的主室中间有一个燃池。家庭成员睡

---

sacred *adj.* 神圣的

on woven grass mats. Fires provided light and heat during cold winter nights.

The Sonoran Supermarket

Like other deserts, the Sonoran Desert can be a difficult place to live. It is hot and dry. Months may pass without any rain. Summer days can reach up to 49° *Celsius* (120°F). Winter nights can dip below freezing.

But as far as deserts go, the Sonoran is *lush* and *hospitable*. The Tohono O'odham lived in an area where 30.5 centimeters (12 in.) of rain fell each year. This was enough rain to support many forms of life. There were shady trees, big cacti, and even summer flowers. Insects, birds, rabbits, and *coyotes* lived there, too.

在用草编织的垫子上。在冬天寒冷的夜里，他们生火来获得光和热。

索诺兰超市

像其他的沙漠一样，索诺兰沙漠也是一个人类居住的险地。这里炎热干燥。几个月下来可能没有一滴雨。夏季这里白天的温度能达到49℃（120华氏度）。冬季夜里的温度能下降到冰点以下。

但就沙漠而言，索诺兰沙漠算是丰茂的，环境也算是宜人的。托何那奥丹人居住的地方每年有30.5厘米（12英寸）的降雨。从维持很多种生命的程度而言，这样的降水已经足够了。这里绿树成荫，有巨型仙人掌，甚至有夏季的繁花。昆虫、鸟类、兔子，还有土狼也生活在这里。

---

celsius *adj.* 摄氏的
hospitable *adj.* （环境）舒适的

lush *adj.* 草木茂盛的
coyote *n.* 丛林狼；草原狼

Some of the O'odham lived near big mountains. There they found *resources* the desert did not have. Different plants and animals lived up in the cooler climate. In the mountains the O'odham gathered food and hunted bigger animals. They also collected water from springs and streams.

A Different Kind of Shopping

If the Tohono O'odham did have a supermarket, t was their desert. When they needed vegetables, they planted seeds. When they needed water, they went to a spring. When they needed meat, they hunted animals. And if they needed pine nuts, they walked up into the mountains to find pine trees.

一些奥丹人生活在大山附近。在那里，他们可以找到沙漠中没有的资源。不同的植物和动物在相对凉爽的气候中快乐地成长。在山区，奥丹人采集食物，猎取更大的动物。他们也从泉水中和小溪中集水。

一种与众不同的购物方式

如果非要说托何那奥丹人有一个超市的话，那么这个超市就是他们所居住的沙漠。当他们需要蔬菜的时候，他们就播下种子；当他们需要水的时候，他们就去泉边；当他们想吃肉的时候，他们就去猎取动物；如果他们需要松子，他们就会走向山中去寻找松树。

---

resource *n.* 资源

Fruits and Vegetables

In the early summer, O'odham men dug small holes in the ground with sharp sticks. Women dropped seeds in each hole and covered them up. These dry fields flooded when the summer rains came. The O'odham grew corn, *beans*, and squash this way. In the winter, they learned to grow wheat, peas, and melons.

Meat

The Tohono O'odham hunted rattlesnakes, rabbits, and birds in the desert. In the mountains, they killed deer, bighorn sheep, and sometimes even bears. To *sneak up* on the deer, O'odham hunters dressed in deerskins and walked on all fours.

果蔬类

夏初时节，奥丹部落的男人开始用尖利的棒子在地上挖小坑。而妇女则将种子播撒到每个小坑里并将其埋上。当夏雨到来的时候，这些干旱的土地将会得以灌溉。奥丹人也用这种方法来种植玉米、豆子和南瓜。冬季，他们学着种植小麦、豌豆和甜瓜。

肉类

托何那奥丹人在沙漠中猎取响尾蛇、兔子和鸟类。在山区，他们猎杀鹿、大角羊，有时甚至是熊。为了偷偷接近鹿，奥丹部落的猎人用鹿皮乔装打扮并爬行前进。

---

bean *n.* 豆；豆子

sneak up 偷偷走近

Organic Specialty Items

The Tohono O'odham also gathered food that grew in the wild. In the desert, they found *chili* peppers, wild onions, *mesquite* beans, and saguaro fruit. In the mountains, they collected *acorns*, roots, and pine nuts. O'odham men even made four-day trips to the ocean to get salt!

Other Native American people wanted these *exotic* foods, too. So the O'odham traded their salt and saguaro syrup for corn, beans, wheat, and more. This extra food helped the O'odham during times of drought.

有机特产

托何那奥丹人也在野外采集食物。沙漠中，他们能够发现红辣椒、野洋葱、牧豆和仙人掌果实。山区里，他们采集橡子、根茎和松子。奥丹人甚至进行4天的旅行到达海边以获取盐！

其他土著人也想要这些具有异国风味的食物。因此，奥丹人用他们的盐和仙人掌果浆换取玉米、小麦和其他食物。这些额外的食物能够帮助奥丹人挨过干旱期。

---

chili *n.* 红辣椒   mesquite *n.* 牧豆树

acorn *n.* 橡子   exotic *adj.* 异国的

Drinking Water

Some O'odham villages were lucky enough to live near springs and streams. Other villages dug wells into the ground. But many people lived far away from water sources. Young girls often traveled high up into mountain canyons to fetch water.

The Bedouin

Think of all the things in your room. Could you imagine moving to a new place every week? Would you get tired of carrying so many things? How would you enjoy the traveling life?

Traditional Bedouin people were nomadic. They moved from place

---

饮用水

一些奥丹人的村庄非常幸运，因为他们住在泉边或小溪附近。其他的村庄在地下打井，但很多人住在离水源很远的地方。年轻的女孩经常翻越高山来到峡谷里取水。

贝都因人

想一想你的房间里都有什么？你能想象到每周都要搬到一个新地方的情景吗？你会不会为带这么多东西感到厌烦？你会怎样享受这样的旅行生活呢？

传统的贝都因人过着游牧生活。他们骑着骆驼流离转徙去寻找食物，

---

traditional *adj.* 传统的

to place on camels in search of food, water, and grazing land. The Bedouin had very few *possessions*. They believed their lifestyle was simple and pure. "Bedouin" means "people of the desert".

The Bedouin lived in low, black tents. These tents protected them from the sun, wind, and blowing sand. In a matter of hours, the Bedouin could pack up their camps and move on to their next "home". Today many Bedouins still roam the Syrian, Arabian, and Sahara deserts.

The Sahara Supermarket?

The Sahara Desert is the largest desert in the world. It stretches across northern Africa for 8 million square kilometers (3.5 million sq. mi.). The Sahara is also very hot and dry. In some parts it rains less

---

水源以及放牧的地方。贝都因人几乎没有什么财产。他们相言他们的生活方式是简单而纯洁的。"贝都因"的意思是"荒原上的游牧民"。

贝都因人住在黑色的低矮帐篷里。这样的帐篷能保护他们不受阳光的暴晒，不受风沙的侵袭。几个小时之内，贝都因人就能将其帐篷收好，搬到另一个新"家"。直至今日，许多贝都因人仍流浪在叙利亚、阿拉伯以及撒哈拉沙漠中。

撒哈拉超市？

撒哈拉沙漠是世界上最大的沙漠。其横跨北非，面积达8,000,000平方公里（3,500,000平方英里）。撒哈拉沙漠也非常炎热干燥。有些地方

---

possession *n.* 财产

than 25 millimeters (1 in.) per year!

The Sahara Desert is less of a "supermarket" than the Sonoran Desert. Less rain falls in the Sahara. This means that fewer plants and animals live there. With few resources available, the Bedouin could not just stay in one place. They had to travel the desert in search of food and water.

The Sahara is more than sand dunes. It also has rocky plateaus, tall mountains, and *oasis* valleys. An oasis is a *fertile* place in the desert where there is water.

The Camel Convenience Store

Arabian camels were the Bedouin's close companions. These *sturdy* animals made nomadic life possible. Camels gave the Bedouin

---

的年降水量甚至不到25厘米（1英寸）！

　　撒哈拉沙漠"超市"比索诺兰沙漠"超市"可差多了。撒哈拉的降水要比索诺兰少。这也就意味着在撒哈拉生长的植物和动物也更少。因为可用的资源少得可怜，贝都因人不可能在一个地方生活一辈子。为了寻找食物和水，他们必须在沙漠中不断迁徙。

　　撒哈拉沙漠并不是只有沙丘。这里也有岩石高原、高山和绿洲山谷。绿洲是沙漠中肥沃的地方，这里有水。

　　骆驼便利店

　　阿拉伯单峰驼是贝都因人的亲密伙伴。这些强健的动物使游牧生活

---

oasis *n.* （沙漠中的）绿洲　　　　　　　　　　　　fertile *adj.* 肥沃的
sturdy *adj.* 结实的；强壮的

shelter, clothing, food, and free rides.

The Bedouin wove camel hair into tents and clothing. They also drank the camels' milk and ate the camels' meat. They even burned the camels' dung to fuel their *campfires*!

Camels were well suited for the desert. They could go for long periods of time without water. Arabian camels could walk for 50 kilometers (30 mi.) in a day. They could also carry up to 270 kilograms (600 lbs.).

Some families owned many camels. Having many camels was a sign of wealth. Camels were so prized that people fought over them. The Bedouin went on raids to steal camels from others.

成为可能。骆驼给贝都因人提供了住所、衣物、食物，还有免费的交通工具。

贝都因人将骆驼毛编织成帐篷和衣物。他们也喝骆驼奶、吃骆驼肉。他们甚至用骆驼粪充当营地篝火的燃料！

骆驼适合生活在沙漠中。它们可以在没有水的情况下行进很长时间。阿拉伯单峰驼一天可以行走50公里（30英里）。它们也可以携带270公斤（600磅）的东西。

有些家庭拥有很多骆驼。拥有很多的骆驼是其富有的象征。骆驼被他们看作是最有价值的东西，有时甚至人们会为骆驼发生争斗。贝都因人会为了从别人那里偷骆驼而进行突袭。

---

campfire *n.* 篝火

Fruits and Vegetables

The nomadic Bedouin did not grow many crops. They were always on the move. But in late summer they camped out near oases because date palms grew there. These trees produced tasty dates. The Bedouin ate some dates fresh and dried others to save for later.

Meat

The Bedouin hunted wild herds of *ostriches*, wolves, foxes, and *gazelles*. They also trained *falcons* to hunt foxes and small birds for them. Sometimes dogs, called salukis, rode with the Bedouin to help track animals. Can you imagine a dog riding on a camel?

果蔬类

游牧的贝都因人并不种植大量的庄稼。他们一直四处奔波。但在晚夏时节，他们会在绿洲附近野营，因为那里长有枣椰树。这些枣椰树会长出美味的海枣。贝都因人会吃掉一些新鲜的海枣，然后会将剩余的晒干留着以后吃。

肉类

贝都因人会将成群的鸵鸟、狼、狐狸还有羚羊当作猎物。他们也会训练猎鹰为其猎取狐狸和小鸟。有时萨卢基狗会与贝都因人同行帮助他们寻找猎物的踪迹。你能想象出一只狗骑在骆驼上会是什么样吗？

---

ostrich *n.* 鸵鸟

falcon *n.* 猎鹰

gazelle *n.* 羚羊

Drinking Water

The Bedouin knew where to find the desert's oases. They dug wells to pull water from the ground. They carried the water in bags made of camel skin.

More Desert People

The Tohono O'odham and the Bedouin are just two of the world's traditional desert peoples. There are many more deserts. And there are many more desert peoples.

The Australian Aborigines, for example, walked about their *continent* for *millennia*. Men hunted with spears and *boomerangs*. Women gathered food. The Aborigines wore very little clothing. They

---

饮用水

贝都因人知道哪里有绿洲。他们挖井以获取地下水。他们用骆驼皮制成的袋子装水。

其他的荒漠人

托何那奥丹人和贝都因人只是世界上传统荒漠人中的两个部落。世界上还有更多的沙漠。在这些沙漠中还有更多的荒漠人。

例如，澳大利亚的土著居民已经在这块陆地上生活了上千年了。男人用矛和回力镖进行猎取活动。妇女则负责采集食物。这些土著居民几乎不

---

continent *n.* 陆地
boomerang *n.* 回力镖

millennium *n.* 一千年（millennia为复数形式）

slept by the warmth of the campfire.

Nomads roamed the cold and windy Gobi Desert. They searched for vegetation for their sheep, goats, and cattle. They lived in yurts, which were like round tents.

The Atacama Indians lived in the dry Atacama Desert. They raised guinea pigs and *llamas*. They also planted crops.

Bushmen lived in the Kalahari Desert. Women gathered plants and roots. Men hunted animals with bows and arrows.

The desert covers rougly one-fifth of the Earth's surface area. Can you find the Sonoran Desert and the Sahara Desert?

穿衣服。他们在温暖的营火边睡觉。

游牧民在寒冷多风的戈壁沙漠中流浪。他们四处寻找植被以饲养他们的绵羊、山羊和牛。他们生活在看起来像圆形帐篷的蒙古包中。

阿塔卡玛印第安人生活在干燥的阿塔卡玛沙漠中。他们饲养豚鼠和大羊驼，他们也种庄稼。

布希曼人生活在卡拉哈里沙漠中。妇女采集植物和根茎，男人用弓箭狩猎。

沙漠覆盖了地球表面约五分之一的面积。你能找到索诺兰沙漠和撒哈拉沙漠吗？

llama *n.* 美洲驼（产于南美）

A Way of Life

Imagine again that you are standing alone in the desert. The sun is now shining over the mountains. The doves have found shade under a tree. You feel a bead of sweat on your *forehead*. What will you do on this day?

If you grew up in the desert, you would know exactly what to do. Your grandparents would have taught your parents. And your parents would have taught you. You would know how to grow vegetables. You would know which wild berries were safe to eat. You would know where to find the well or the closest spring.

生活之道

再想象一下你独自一人伫立在沙漠中的情景。阳光洒满了高山。鸽子也找到了树荫。你的额头上渗出了一滴汗水。今天你要做些什么呢？

如果你在沙漠中长大，你就会知道要做什么。你的祖父母会教你的父母，你的父母也同样会教你。你会知道如何种菜。你会知道哪种野草莓吃起来是安全的。你会知道在哪儿能找到井或最近的泉眼。

---

forehead *n.* 额

For thousands of years, people have adapted to deserts. They have found food, water, shelter, and more. For these people, the desert is not just about *survival*. It is their way of life.

Digging Deeper

Did you find the stories of the Tohono O'odham and Bedouin interesting? Would you like to read more about them? There are many other interesting desert peoples, too. Go ahead and take a look.

几千年来，人们已经适应了沙漠中的生活。他们已经找到了食物、水、住所，甚至更多。对这些人来说，沙漠的意义不仅仅是求生，这是他们的生活之道。

深入探究

你认为托何那奥丹部落和贝都因人的故事有趣吗？是否愿意阅读更多关于他们的故事？除了他们，还有很多其他能让人产生兴趣的荒漠人。接着看吧。

---

survival *n.* 生存

1. At the Library

Tell your librarian you want to read about people who live in deserts. You could also ask for books about deserts themselves.

2. On the Web

A. In the address window, type: www.google.com

B. Then type: desert people. Click on "Google Search".

C. Read the colored links. Click on one that looks interesting.

D. When you want to *explore* other links, click the back arrow at the top left of the screen.

E. Or try some different searches: Tohono O'odham, Bedouin, Sonoran Desert, Sahara Desert, or world deserts.

---

1. 图书馆内

告诉图书管理员你想读些关于生活在沙漠中的人们的故事。你也可以找一些介绍沙漠本身的书籍。

2. 上网浏览

A. 在地址窗口键入：www.google.com。

B. 然后键入：沙漠人，点击"谷歌地球"。

C. 阅读彩色链接。点击看起来有趣的那一个。

D. 如果你想探索其他链接，点击屏幕左上角的后退箭头。

E. 也可以试一试一些不同的搜索：托何那奥丹、贝都因人、索诺兰沙漠、撒哈拉沙漠或世界上的沙漠。

---

explore *v.* 探索

04

The Inuit: Northern Living

Inuit Words in English

Many Inuit spoke a language called Inuktitut. Some of the words they used are now words that we use in English.

igloo: a dome-shaped house built from blocks of snow

kayak: a light and narrow boat, like a canoe but with a covered **deck**

parka: a warm, **hooded** *jacket*

因纽特人：北方的生活

因纽特的英语词汇

许多因纽特人说着一种叫作因纽特语的语言。他们使用的其中一些词汇是我们现在所使用的英语词汇。

伊格鲁：用雪块建成的圆拱形房屋

海豹皮船：轻巧狭窄的小船，类似独木舟，但有甲板覆盖

派克大衣：一种保暖的连帽夹克

deck *n.* 甲板   hooded *adj.* 带有风帽的

The Frozen North

There is a place on Earth where it is always cold. The ground is frozen and the land is flat. For much of the year, it is covered in a white blanket of snow.

This land is so far north that during the winter, the sun doesn't come above the horizon. The land remains dark twenty-four hours a day. But during the summer, the sun is always above the *horizon*. It is light outside twenty-four hours a day. That's why this place, the *Arctic*, is sometimes called "the Land of the Midnight Sun".

If you visit the Arctic region, you'll feel how cold it is. The temperature on an average winter day is about –34° Celsius (–30° F)!

冰封北国

地球上有这么一个地方，这里一年四季冰冷刺骨。这里地面结冰，地表平坦。全年的大部分时间，这里都是一片皑皑白雪。

这里是遥远的北方，冬季时节，太阳甚至不能升上地平线。这里一天二十四小时都是漆黑的。但在夏季的时候，太阳却是一直在地平线以上的。这时的北极一天二十四小时都是阳光普照。这就是这个地方——北极——有时被称为"午夜太阳之地"。

如果你去了北极地区，你就会感觉到这里有多么寒冷。这里冬季的平均温度为-34摄氏度（-30华氏度）！每年，这里有38到229厘米（15至90

horizon *n.* 地平线   Arctic *n.* 北极

Each year, between 38 and 229 centimeters (15–90 in.) of snow fall. For many months, the Arctic's rivers, lakes, and seas freeze over. Brrr!

So if it's that cold and snowy, how can anything survive in the Arctic? The land is mostly barren tundra where even trees cannot grow. But some plants can take root in the far north. These are low-growing *mosses*, shrubs, and tiny flowering plants.

Animals have also found ways to live in the Arctic. Salmon, lake *trout*, and Arctic cod are fish that swim in the cold waters. Whales, seals, *walruses*, and polar bears live in and around the sea. Layers of fat beneath their skin serves as warm insulation. Wolves, foxes,

---

英寸）的降雪。好几个月的时间，北极的河流、湖泊、海洋都被冰封了。哎呀，好冷啊！

那么既然这里这么寒冷多雪，生物怎能在这里活下去呢？这里大部分是贫瘠的苔原地带，树木甚至不能在这里生长。但有些植物却能植根于此。这些植物都是些长得很低的苔藓、灌木，还有很小的开花植物。

动物在北极也找到了生活的方法。鲑鱼、湖红点鲑、北极鳕鱼都是生活在冰冷水域的鱼类。鲸鱼、海豹、海象，还有北极熊也生活在这片水域或在大海附近。这些动物皮下的脂肪层就是防寒的保温层。狼、狐狸，还

---

moss *n.* 苔藓　　　　　　　　　　　　trout *n.* 鳟鱼
walrus *n.* 海象

and *caribou* roam the *tundra*. Their thick coats of fur help keep them warm. In the summertime, ducks and geese migrate to the Arctic to build nests and raise their young.

So if plants and animals can survive in the far north, what about people? How would you stay warm during the cold, dark winters? How would you stay protected from the icy winds and snowstorms? How would you find food?

People have lived in and near the Arctic for thousands of years. Before there were stores, fancy jackets, or electricity, these people survived in the frozen north. They built houses from *driftwood*, earth,

---

有北美驯鹿漫步在这片苔原上。它们厚厚的毛皮能够帮助它们保暖。夏季时节，鸭、鹅迁徙到了北极开始筑巢繁衍下一代。

既然植物和动物能在遥远的北极生存，那么人类可以吗？你如何在寒冷黑暗的冬天取暖？如何才能不受冰冷的寒风还有暴风雪的侵袭？如何去寻找食物？

人类已经在北极及其附近生活了上千年了。在有商店、精致的夹克，或电之前，这些人就早已在冰封的北国开始生活了。他们用浮木、泥土、鲸鱼骨，还有雪来建造房屋。他们穿着动物皮勇敢地面对着严寒。生活在

---

caribou *n.* 北美驯鹿

driftwood *n.* 浮木

tundra *n.* 苔原

whalebones, and snow. They burned whale fat to heat their homes. And they wore animal skins and fur to brave the harsh cold. The hearty people of the far north of North America used to be commonly known as "the Eskimo", but we now know them by their preferred name, the Inuit .

The Inuit are Native Americans. This means that their ancestors lived in North America since long before Europeans came to the Americas. Over time, the Inuit spread out to live in many different areas. Some of them lived just south of the Arctic where there were trees. There, they could build houses out of wood. But many Inuit

---

北美洲遥远的北方的这些健壮的人们过去通常被称为"爱斯基摩人",但现在我们用他们比较喜欢的名字——因纽特人来称呼他们。

因纽特人是美洲原住民。也就是说在欧洲人来到美洲很早以前,他们的祖先就生活在北美洲了。随着时间的流逝,因纽特人生活的范围扩大到了许多不同的地区。有些因纽特人生活在北极圈以南的地方,这里生长着树木。在这里,他们可以用木材建造房屋。但很多因纽特人还是居住在朝

---

whalebone *n.* 鲸鱼骨

lived far to the north, where there were no trees. They built houses of whale bones, hides, earth, and they sometimes built shelters out of hardpacked snow.

This story is about the traditional way the Inuit lived. It does not describe how every Inuit person lived, but gives an *overview* of how many of them lived for many years. You will read about igloos, dogsleds, ice fishing, and more. You will even find out what games the Inuit played on cold winter days. And in the last chapter, you will read about the Inuit who still live in the far north today.

向北方的遥远地方，这里没有树木生长。他们用鲸鱼骨、动物皮、泥土建造房屋，有时甚至用压实的雪块搭建住所。

这个故事讲述了因纽特人的传统生活方式。这里并没有描述每个因纽特人是怎样生活的，但却概述了有多少人在这里生活了这么多年。你将读到有关伊格鲁、狗拉雪橇、冰下捕鱼等更多的知识。你甚至可以了解因纽特人在寒冷的冬季都玩什么游戏。在最后一章里，你还会对现今仍生活在遥远的北极的因纽特人有所了解。

overview *n.* 概述

Many People, Many Names

For many years, all northern Native Americans were called "Eskimo." But many tribes do not like this name because it was given to them by other tribes, some of whom were their enemies. Eskimo means "eater of raw meat". Some Alaskan tribes still call themselves Eskimo, but most northern people prefer the general term "Inuit". Some people prefer their specific *tribal name, rather than a general name. And tribes in Siberia are not called Inuit. They have their own names.*

很多人，很多名字

许多年来，所有的北方美洲原住民都被叫作"爱斯基摩人"。但很多部落并不喜欢这个名字，因为这个名字是其他部落赋予的，有些部落甚至是他们的敌人。爱斯基摩的意思是"吃生肉的人"。一些阿拉斯加部落仍称自己为爱斯基摩人，但大部分生活在北极的人们喜欢"因纽特人"这个泛称。有些人喜欢他们自己特定的部落名称，而不是通用名称。生活在西伯利亚的部落就不叫做因纽特人。他们有自己的名字。

specific *adj.* 特定的

Staying Warm

The Inuit knew how to stay warm in freezing conditions. For clothing, they wore the skins of Arctic animals. Inuit women cleaned these skins and sewed them into pants, socks, boots, and gloves. The most important article of clothing was the *parka*, which was a thick, hooded jacket.

Caribou skin was a popular material because it was lightweight, yet warm. When there wasn't caribou skin, the Inuit used skins from foxes, seals, and polar bears. They decorated their clothing with beads and carvings. Some Inuit used *goggles* to protect their eyes from "snow blindness", or eye damage from the harsh sunlight

取暖

因纽特人知道如何在冰冷的条件下取暖。他们将北极动物的外皮当作衣服。因纽特妇女将这些外皮清洗干净，然后将其缝制成裤子、袜子、靴子，还有手套。服装中最重要的物品是派克大衣——一种厚厚的带帽子的夹克。

北美驯鹿皮是一种比较受欢迎的材料，因为它虽然重量轻，但却很保暖。没有驯鹿皮的时候，因纽特人就会使用狐狸皮、海豹皮和北极熊皮制衣。他们用珠子和雕刻品装饰自己的衣服。一些因纽特人会使用护目镜以防止患上"雪盲症"，或者因从白色冰雪反射过来刺眼的阳光而受的眼

parka *n.* 派克大衣；风雪外套   goggles *n.* 护目镜

reflecting off the white snow and ice. They carved these goggles out of wood and bone. Then they cut small slits to see through. These goggles worked like sunglasses.

Inuit houses were an *essential* part of staying warm. The Inuit used the best building materials they could find in their environment. Some Inuit were lucky enough to have driftwood, rocks, and *sod*. Caribou skins helped to insulate the walls. To heat and light the insides of their homes, the Inuit burned oil lamps. This oil came from melted animal fat, usually from seals, walruses, or whales. The lamps' wicks were made of moss and grass.

伤。他们用木材或骨头雕刻护目镜，通过在上面切割的狭窄的小缝向外界看。他们所制作的护目镜实际上起到了太阳镜的作用。

　　因纽特人的房屋是其防寒不可或缺的一部分。因纽特人使用在他们生存的环境中能找到的最好的建筑材料。如果有浮木、岩石和草皮的话，这对因纽特人来说再幸运不过了。驯鹿皮能帮助他们房屋的墙不透风。因纽特人点燃油灯来给屋内带来暖气和光亮。油灯里的油来自于溶化后的动物脂肪，通常是海豹、海象或鲸鱼的脂肪。灯芯是由苔藓或草制成的。

---

essential *adj.* 必不可少的　　　　　　　　　　　sod *n.* 草皮

When the Inuit could not find wood, rocks, or sod during the long and snowy winter, they used snow and ice to build houses. People today call these snow houses igloos. Most people are *fascinated* by igloos. Not many of us can imagine living in a house built just from blocks of ice and snow. Wouldn't it be like living in a freezer? And wouldn't an igloo melt from the heat inside?

Some Inuit lived in igloos all winter long. These igloos were so tall that adults could stand up inside them. People slept, ate, and gathered in the igloo's main room. Many igloos had side rooms for storage. And sometimes underground *passageways* connected neighboring igloos.

The weather outside was so cold that igloos did not melt in the

在漫长多雪的冬季，当因纽特人不能够找到木材、岩石或草皮的时候，他们就会用雪和冰建造房屋。今天人们将这样的雪屋叫作伊格鲁。大多数人都会被伊格鲁所深深吸引。很少人会想象出住在由冰块和雪块建造的房屋内是什么样的。不会像是住在冰箱里吧？里面的热气不会使伊格鲁融化？

一些因纽特人整个冬天都住在伊格鲁里。伊格鲁足够高到成人在里面能够直立。人们在伊格鲁的主室里睡觉，吃饭，聚会。很多伊格鲁都有存储用的厢房。有时地下通道会连接到附近的伊格鲁。

外部的天气非常寒冷以至于伊格鲁不会在冬季融化。但在里面，伊格

fascinate *v.* 使着迷　　　　　　　　　　passageway *n.* 通道

winter. But on the inside, igloos could be quite warm. Long entrance *tunnels* (just big enough to crawl through) kept out the wind and the cold. Oil lamps, cooking fires, and body heat warmed up the main room. Adults and kids slept on snow *platforms* covered with animal skin. Some igloos had "windows" made from clear lake ice. Caribou or seal skins lined the inside walls and kept the snow and ice from melting by trapping the heat inside.

Venturing Out for Food

The Inuit developed creative ways of traveling. In the winter, teams of dogs pulled sleds through the snow. The sleds rested on skis made from wood and whalebone. In the summer, the Inuit walked over land to gather berries, *seaweed*, bird eggs, and wild

---

鲁却是非常温暖的。很长的入口隧道（人们刚刚能够爬行穿过）将大风和严寒挡在了外面。油灯、烹饪用火，还有身体的热量让整个主室变得暖和起来。大人和孩子睡在用雪做成的平台上，上面覆盖着一层动物皮。有些伊格鲁有用清澈的湖冰做成的"窗户"。驯鹿皮或海豹皮被做成了墙的内衬，这样的话屋内的热量就不会使冰雪融化了。

为寻找食物去探险

因纽特人开发出了具有创造性的旅行方式。冬季，成群结队的狗拉着雪橇穿行在雪地上。安装在滑雪板上的雪橇是用木材和鲸鱼骨制成的。夏

---

tunnel n. 隧道 platform n. 平台
seaweed n. 海藻

vegetables.

When the winter ice *thawed*, the Inuit also traveled by boat. A common boat for one or two people was called a kayak. Kayaks were like narrow canoes with covered tops. Paddlers sat in small openings. They attached *waterproof* jackets made of seal *intestine* around the edges of the openings to prevent water from getting inside. Kayaks were made so wellbalanced that if they tipped, paddlers could easily roll over until they were rightside-up again.

The frozen tundra ground was not good for growing crops like corn, beans, or wheat. There were no stores to buy goods. *Therefore*, the Inuit had to travel by foot, sled, and boat to find food.

季，因纽特人行走在陆地上去采集浆果、海藻、鸟蛋和野菜。

当冬季的寒冰溶解后，因纽特人开始乘船旅行。一艘供一人或两人乘坐的普通船只被人们称为"海豹皮船"。海豹皮船类似于一种上面被覆盖了的独木舟。船桨手坐在狭小的开口内。他们在开口的周围裹上用海豹肠制成的防水套，这样就能防止船体进水。海豹皮船具有极好的平衡性，如果皮船翻倒的话，船桨手可以轻松地翻转过来直至船体重新正面朝上。

冰冻的苔原地并不适合像玉米、豆子或小麦这样的庄稼生长。这里也没有能够购物的商店。因此，因纽特人必须以步行、乘雪橇、划船这样的方式去寻找食物。大部分的食物都是通过狩猎和捕鱼获得的。

thaw *v.* 融化
intestine *n.* 肠

waterproof *adj.* 防水的
therefore *adv.* 因此

They found most of their food by hunting and fishing.

Sometimes the Inuit hunted on land, and other times they hunted on the sea. Seals and caribou were their primary targets. Hunters used *harpoons*, darts tipped with poison, and bows and arrows. They speared whales, caught foxes in traps, and fished through holes in the ice.

But the resourceful Inuit didn't kill animals just for food. They used all parts of the animals to make tools, weapons, clothing, and shelter. For example, when the Inuit killed a whale, they first ate its meat. Then they melted the whale fat into oil to heat and light their homes. Finally, the Inuit carved knives and tools out of whalebone.

　　有时因纽特人会在陆地上狩猎，其他时候也在海上狩猎。海豹和北美驯鹿是他们的主要目标。猎人将鱼叉、蘸有毒药的飞镖，还有弓箭作为狩猎工具。他们用长矛刺杀鲸鱼、用陷阱抓捕狐狸、在冰窟窿边进行捕鱼。

　　但机智的因纽特人不仅仅将猎杀的动物作为食物。他们使用动物的各个部分制作工具、武器、衣服，还有住所。例如，当因纽特人杀死一只鲸鱼的时候，他们先吃掉它的肉。然后他们将鲸鱼的脂肪溶化成油作为房屋中用来取暖和照明的燃料。最后，因纽特人用鲸鱼骨雕刻成刀和其他工具。

---

harpoon *n.* 鱼叉

Inuit Resource Menu		
Animal	*Food*	*Other Uses*
Whale	*Whale meat*	• *fat for light, heat, and cooking* • *bones for knives*
Seal	*Seal meat*	• *skins for boots* • *intestines to waterproof kayaks*
Caribou	*Caribou meat*	• *skins for warm parkas* • *skins to sleep on*
Walrus	*Walrus meat*	• *skins for blankets* • *ivory tusks for carvings*

因纽特人的资源列单		
动物	食物	其他用途
鲸鱼	鲸鱼肉	• 脂肪用作照明、取暖、烹饪 • 骨头用作制造刀具
海豹	海豹肉	• 海豹皮用作制作靴子 • 肠子用作制造防水的海豹皮船
北美驯鹿	驯鹿肉	• 驯鹿皮用作缝制温暖的派克大衣 • 可以睡在驯鹿皮上
海象	海象肉	• 海象皮用作制造毯子 • 海象牙用来制成雕刻品

ivory *n.* 象牙

Work and Play

Inuit men spent much of their time hunting, fishing, and making tools. Women often cooked, skinned animals, and sewed skins into clothing. The kids helped out with these chores until they were old enough to do them alone. There was no such thing as "school" for kids.

The Inuit enjoyed playing games and using their *imaginations*. Harsh winter storms could keep them inside for days at a time. So people told stories, sang songs, danced, and played drums made of animal skin. Sometimes they even wrestled and played *tug-of-war*.

Kids played with dolls, bows and arrows, and leather balls. They

---

工作和娱乐

因纽特男人将大量的时间用于狩猎、捕鱼以及制作工具。妇女则通常负责做饭、剥动物皮并将动物皮缝制成衣服。孩子们是这些家务活的帮手，直至他们年龄足够大到可以独立完成这些工作。这里没有专门为孩子准备的如"学校"之类的事物。

因纽特人喜欢做游戏并利用他们的想象力。严冬的风暴能使他们一连几天待在屋里不能出门。所以人们就讲故事、唱歌、跳舞、敲动物皮制成的鼓。有时他们甚至摔跤、拔河。

孩子们玩玩偶、弓箭，还有皮球。他们也用看起来像动物的雕刻品装

---

imagination *n.* 想象   tug-of-war *n.* 拔河

also decorated pins, combs, and goggles with carvings that looked like animals. Fathers often made "story knives" for their daughters. Girls used these story knives to draw pictures in the snow and dirt. They sat in circles with friends and made up stories based on the pictures.

Surely one of the favorite games for kids was the "blanket toss". In this game, one person lay on a blanket made from walrus hides. Then all at once, everybody pulled the blanket tight. This was like a *trampoline* that sent people flying into the air! Sometimes they landed on their feet, and other times they did flips.

The Inuit Today

In the last three sections, you read about traditional Inuit ways

饰发夹、梳子和护目镜。父亲通常会为女儿制作"故事刀"。女孩用故事刀在雪中或泥土上画画。她们与朋友们环圈而坐并根据这些图画编故事。

可以肯定的是，其中最受孩子们欢迎的一个游戏就算是"跳毯子"了。在这个游戏中，一个人躺在由海象皮制成的毯子上面，然后突然间每个人将毯子拉紧，这就像蹦床一样将人弹向空中！有时毯子上的人会双脚着地，有时会在毯子上翻空翻。

今天的因纽特人

上面的三部分，我们了解到了因纽特人的传统生活方式。他们当中的

trampoline *n.* 蹦床

of living. This is how many of them lived for thousands of years. Yet over the last few hundred years, things have changed. Today there are airports, TVs, and computers in the Arctic.

Now the Inuit are trying to find a *balance* between the modern world and traditional ways. Many Inuit prefer houses with electricity instead of dark igloos. But modern houses cost money. And to make money, Inuit people have to find jobs. This means that many Inuit spend their days at jobs other than hunting and fishing. There are also fewer wild animals than before. This makes it harder to hunt.

Today, land in the frozen north is divided between different countries. The Inuit live in the northern parts of Canada, Greenland, Russia, and the United States. In 1999 Canada made a *territory* for

---

许多人用这种方式生活了上千年。但在最近的几百年时间里，很多事情发生了改变。现如今，北极也有机场、电视，还有电脑。

当前，因纽特人正在现代世界和传统方式之间寻找一种平衡。很多因纽特人喜欢电气化的房屋而不是黑暗的伊格鲁。但现代的房屋是需要花钱的。为了赚钱，因纽特人不得不出去找工作。也就是说许多因纽特人将时间花费到了工作上而不是狩猎和捕鱼。而且现在野生动物也不如从前多了，这也让狩猎变得更加困难。

如今，冰封的北极地区被分成了不同的国家。因纽特人生活在加拿大、格陵兰、俄罗斯以及美国的北部。1999年，加拿大为因纽特人建立

---

balance *n.* 平衡　　　　　　　　　　territory *n.* 地区

the Inuit called Nunavut. Nunavut means "Our Land". Its official languages are Inuktitut, English, and French.

Now there are also schools in the Arctic. Children spend their days reading and writing instead of fishing and sewing. Inuit elders sometimes visit schools to teach the children Inuit traditions. They help students carve wood, sew animal skins, and tell stories. The elders want kids to remember how their ancestors lived for thousands of years.

If you visited the far north today, you would need to *bundle up*. Maybe you'd wear a warm jacket, or two or three. If you went in the wintertime, it would be dark in the middle of the day. It would be

了自治区，命名为努纳武特。努纳武特的意思是"我们的土地"，其官方语言为因纽特语，英语和法语。

现在在北极也有学校。孩子们不再以捕鱼和缝纫度过时光，取而代之的是读书写字。一些因纽特的长辈有时会去学校教授这些孩子们因纽特的传统。他们帮助学生在木头上雕刻、缝制动物皮、讲故事。长辈们想要孩子们记住他们的祖先是如何生活了数以千年的。

如果你现在去遥远的北极，你可能需要穿暖和些。也许你会穿一件保暖夹克，或两件，或三件。如果你是在冬季去的，那里每一天都将是漆黑

bundle up 　（使）穿得暖和

freezing cold for days and weeks and months. A visit to the Arctic might make you wonder how people can survive in such a harsh *environment*.

During your visit, you would meet Inuit people. You would see how they have blended traditional ways with modern living. For example, you might see an Inuit man wearing blue jeans and a caribou skin parka. You might ride on a sled that is pulled by a snowmobile instead of dogs. Or you might see seal hunters wearing sunglasses instead of wooden goggles. And before going home, you might buy a piece of Inuit art, such as a little animal carved out of stone. It would be a *souvenir* to help you remember your visit to the far north.

一片。这里几天、几周，甚至几个月都会滴水成冰。去北极旅行可能会使你对人们如何在如此恶劣的环境下生存感到惊讶。

游览的时候，你可能会遇到因纽特人。你会看到他们是如何将传统方式同现代生活融合到一起的。例如，你可能看到穿着蓝色牛仔裤搭配一件驯鹿皮派克大衣的因纽特男子。你可能骑在由雪地机动车拖着的雪橇上面，而不是狗拉雪橇。或者你可能看到海豹猎人戴着一副太阳镜，而不是木制护目镜。回家之前，你可能会买一件因纽特艺术品，如用石头雕刻的小动物。这将会是一件帮助你记住你的北极之旅的纪念品。

---

environment *n.* 环境   souvenir *n.* 纪念品

05

Otzi: The Iceman

About 5,300 Years Ago

The man gently pushed aside the small brown dog yapping at his feet, tipping the basket of grain he was carrying just enough to *spill*. "Now see what a mess you've made." He smiled at the puppy through his *irritation*.

The man knew he had a lot to do to get ready for the hunt. He had no time to waste, as winter was closing in.

冰人奥茨

大约5300年前

男人温和地把脚边狂叫的棕色小狗推到一边，这让他肩上扛着的那篮子谷物倾斜了一下，洒到了地上一些。"看看你闯的祸。"他嗔怪着小狗。

男人出发打猎前还有很多准备要作。他不能浪费时间，因为冬天就要到了。

---

spill *v.* （使）洒出；泼出

irritation *n.* 恼怒

A tall, dark-haired boy walked over to the area of spilled grain and began scooping it up.

The man looked upon his son with pride. "You must take care of things while I'm gone."

"Yes, Father. I know."

Together, father and son placed the grain back in the basket while the dog played at their *heels*. The boy took the grain to an underground pit where it would be protected during the *upcoming* winter.

The man and his son walked slowly back to their home. The man paused to stop and rub his legs.

一个高高的黑头发男孩走到谷物洒落的地方，开始用铲子捡谷物。

男人骄傲地看着自己的儿子说："我不在家的时候，你要照顾好家里的一切。"

"好的，爸爸。我知道。"

父子俩一起把谷子收回了篮子里，那只狗在他们的脚边玩耍。男孩把谷子放进了一个埋在地下的罐子里，这样，这些谷子在冬天才能保存完好。

男人和他的儿子慢慢地走回了家。男人时不时地停下来搓搓他的腿。

---

heel *n.* 脚后跟   upcoming *adj.* 即将来到的

He knew the weather would soon turn colder, which would make food *scarcer*.

Tension would be high in the community as men who weren't able to kill enough on the hunt fought over food for their families. It was important for him to leave the village soon and hunt for red deer, ibex, and wild boar. His family would need to live off the meat during the winter.

When the man returned home, he gathered his *belongings* together. He knew he needed to be prepared to face almost anything. Then he left his family and began his journey.

Traveling only a short distance from his home, the man killed an ibex and was carrying the meat. All of a sudden, an arrow whizzed

---

他知道天气很快就会变冷了，将会很难找到食物。

如果男人们不能打到充足的猎物作为家人过冬的食物，村子里局势就会很紧张。对他来说，重要的是马上离开村庄，去猎捕赤鹿、野羊和野猪。他的家人需要靠着这些肉过冬。

男人回到家里，带上他的装备。他知道他得作好万全的准备。然后，他离开家人，去捕猎了。

走到离家不远的地方，男人杀死了一只野羊，他把肉扛在了肩上。突然，一支箭从男人的耳边飞过。接着又射过来几支。其中一支射中了男人

---

scarce *adj.* 缺乏的   belongings *n.* 动产；财物

by the man's ear. Then several more flew through the air, and one landed sharply in the back of the man's right shoulder.

The man *clutched* his arm in pain. Moaning, he reached behind with his left hand to *withdraw* the arrow but could not remove it entirely. He managed to walk slowly up a hill as he heard the men behind him taking the bundle of meat he'd dropped. Making it to the hilltop, he lay down and closed his eyes for the last time.

Little did the man know that his body would become frozen in ice and frozen in time, and that thousands of years later he would become known as Otzi, the Iceman.

Of course, this is just one possible way that Otzi, the Iceman, died. We really don't know for sure how it happened. All we can do

---

的右肩后面。

男人痛苦地抓着手臂，呻吟着，他伸出左手去拔箭，可是根本够不到。听到身后的人抬走了他刚刚掉在地上的肉，他设法一点一点向山上挪动。刚走到了山顶，他就躺在了地上，永远地合上了眼睛。

这个男人绝对不会知道他的尸体会成为冰尸，没多久就冻成了冰。并且几千年后，他会成为众所周知的冰人奥茨。

当然，这只是对冰人奥茨死亡的一种可能的猜测。我们实际上并不了解事情的真相。我们只能在一些事实的基础上，对他的死进行推测和猜

---

clutch v. 抓紧　　　　　　　　　　　withdraw v. 拿走；撤走

is *theorize*, or make guesses based on the facts. Scientists collect facts—clues—before they make a theory. You can make a theory about how Otzi died, too. As you read the things we do know, think like a scientist and come up with your own theories.

Finding the Iceman

In September 1991, two German hikers, Erika and Helmut Simon, made an amazing discovery. High in the Tyrolean Alps, at more than 10,000 feet, near the border between Austria and Italy, they found a hairless, frozen body. Only the head and part of the shoulders could be seen above the ice.

想。科学家们在假想前要收集证据——也就是线索。你也可以对奥茨的死亡原因提出自己的假说。了解了我们掌握的证据后，你也可以像科学家一样，提出自己的猜想。

发现冰人

1991年9月，两个德国的徒步旅行者——西蒙夫妇共同发现了这个神奇的冰人。在提洛尔人居住的阿尔卑斯山上，海拔超过一万英尺的高度，奥地利和意大利的边界附近，西蒙夫妇发现了这具没有头发的冰尸。冰面上面只能看到头和一部分肩膀。

---

theorize *v.* 从理论上说明

They *originally* thought it was the frozen *corpse* of a modern climber. However, a few days later, Austrian scientist Rainer Henn came up with a different theory. The corpse was yellowed and dried, so he determined that it must have been frozen for a long time. He was right. The Iceman turned out to be about 5,000 years old.

The Man Himself

Scientists used carbon dating, *microscopic* analysis, and X-rays on the Iceman's well-preserved body to gather clues about his *appearance* and physical condition. They determined that Otzi was short—only about five feet tall—weighed about 110 pounds, had wavy brown hair, and probably wore a beard.

　　他们原本以为是现代登山者的尸体。然而，几天后，奥地利科学家莱尼亨恩给出了不同的说法。尸体颜色发黄并且已经风干，因此，他断定尸体已经被冰封很久了。他说得对。冰人被证明已经大约五千岁了。

　　冰人的自身情况

　　科学家们通过碳测，显微分析和X光对这个保存完好的冰人进行检测，收集到了他的体貌特征。他们断定奥茨个子不高——大概只有5英尺。体重大约110磅，棕色卷发，可能还留着胡子。

---

originally *adv.* 起初　　　　　　corpse *n.* 尸体
microscopic *adj.* 显微镜的　　　appearance *n.* 外貌

They also figured out that he lived to be about 46 years old (an elder for that time) and was bothered by several medical conditions: a bad back, *arthritis*, *worn joints*, and a bad stomach.

From Otzi's teeth, scientists were able to theorize about his diet. He probably ate mostly bread because his teeth were ground down, as they could only be from eating grains for many years, but he probably also *consumed* crab apples, berries, acorns, hazelnuts, and the meat of whatever animals he could hunt and kill.

Using these clues and others, scientists began to theorize how Otzi may have died.

他们也推断出了他的年龄，大概活到46岁（那个时代已经算长寿的了）。冰人也有一些病痛：背部疾病，关节炎，关节劳损，还患有严重的胃病。

通过奥茨的牙齿情况，科学家们能推断出他的饮食结构。他的主要饮食可能是面食，因为他的牙齿磨得很平，只有多年食用谷子才能形成这样平整的牙齿。不过他也许还会食用野果、浆果、橡子、榛子还有猎捕到的任何肉类。

基于这些线索还有另外一些发现，科学家们开始推断奥茨的死因。

---

arthritis *n.* 关节炎
joint *n.* 关节

worn *adj.* 磨损的
consume *v.* 吃；喝

Evidence Found With the Iceman

Copper ax

Bow

Arrows, one with traces of blood from two people

Quiver for arrows

Knife, with traces of blood from another person

Grass *sheath* for knife

Strips of felt

Birch bark container

Flint

Wood–frame backpack

Wooden stick with deer antler tip

Bone awl

Cuts on Otzi's hands and wrists

Ibex (wild goat) meat

Sloe berry

Stone disk on a leather string with fringe

Mushrooms tied on a leather string

Tests revealing that Otzi likely had arthritis and suffered from back pain

Long–sleeved jacket or vest made from animal hides, with traces of blood from another person

Woven grass cloak

Leather pouch

Leather pants

Waterproof shoes

Fur hat

Grass socks

Tattoos

已发现的关于奥茨的证据

铜斧

弓箭（其中一支上发现了两个人的血迹）

箭袋

刀（上面有另一个人的血迹）

草编刀鞘

毡子的碎片

桦树皮做的包

坚硬的石头

木制背包

鹿角头木头拐杖

骨锥

奥茨手和手腕上的割伤

野羊肉

一只浆果

皮绳穿着的碟形石坠

用皮绳串着的蘑菇

证明奥茨有关节炎和后背痛的检验结果

动物皮毛做的长袖衣服（有其他人的血迹）

草编斗篷

皮囊

皮裤

防水鞋

皮帽

草袜

文身

sheath *n.* 鞘

tattoo *n.* 文身

At first, *investigators* thought the Iceman got caught in a storm, fell asleep, and died from the cold. But later theories seem to support the idea that the Iceman was killed. Blood was found on Otzi's clothes, and wounds were discovered on his body. A number of scientists believe that the evidence supports the theory that the Iceman died from an arrow wound to his back and knife wounds to his hands. But why? Why would someone want to kill Otzi? There are several theories.

Theory 1: An Accident

While Otzi was hunting, he was *accidentally* shot by other hunters and then buried.

最初，调查者认为冰人遇到了暴风雪，睡着了，死于风寒。但是后来的推断都倾向于认为奥茨是被人杀害的。奥茨衣服上有血迹，身上有伤口。许多科学家都认为这些证据能证明冰人死于背部的箭伤和手上的刀伤。但是为什么呢？为什么会有人想杀害奥茨呢？关于这个问题，有着几种不同的推断。

推断一：意外

当时奥茨正在打猎，其他猎人不小心射死了他，然后把他埋葬了。

---

investigator *n.* 调查者　　　　　accidentally *adv.* 意外地

Scientists think that Otzi was hunting because of the clothing he was wearing and the equipment he was carrying when they found him frozen in the glacier.

From the many *scraps* of *material* they found (leather, fur, grass, bearskin, cowhide, tree bark) on his body, scientists think that the Iceman wore leather pants and a long-sleeved jacket or vest made of deer, goat, and ibex hide, with the fur side turned out, and possibly a long, woven grass cloak.

They guess from the clues that his shoes were waterproof and wide—seemingly designed for walking across the snow—constructed by using bearskin for the soles, cowhide or deer for the

---

科学家们猜想奥茨正在打猎，是因为人们在冰川中找到冰冻的他时，他穿的衣服和携带的物品。

科学家们根据找到的奥茨身上的物品碎片（皮革、毛皮、草、牛皮和树皮），推断冰人当时可能穿着皮裤、长袖外衣或者鹿皮、山羊皮制成的毛面朝外的坎肩，也许还穿了一件草编斗篷。

他的鞋是防水的并且很宽，鞋底看起来是用熊皮做的，鞋面是用鹿皮或牛皮做的，用来缝鞋的线是树皮。他们认为包在奥茨脚周围的软草相当

---

scrap *n.* 碎片 · material *n.* 材料

top panels, and netting made of tree bark. They think soft grass was wound around his feet to function like warm socks. Grass laces, kept dry by a leather flap, were strung through *eyeholes* to keep Otzi's size-six feet snug.

Scientists also theorize that the Iceman wore a hat that was made of individual cut pieces of fur, probably bearskin, sewn together. Attached to the hat were two leather straps that might have been used as a *chinstrap*.

These articles of clothing, scientists think, would be what one would wear going on a long trek, like a hunting expedition. This belief was *reinforced* by the type of equipment Otzi had with him.

于袜子。用草做成的鞋带，上面有一个皮制的封套以保持干燥，这种鞋带穿在鞋帮的洞里，就制成了奥茨的鞋，为他6号的脚保暖。

科学家们也推测冰人可能还带着一顶用熊皮碎片手工缝制的帽子。帽子上还有两个皮片，就像用头巾一样。

科学家们认为这样的衣物是远行者所必需的穿戴，比如说要去狩猎。奥茨随身携带的物品也进一步证明了这一论断。

---

eyehole *n.* 小孔　　　　　　　　　　　　chinstrap *n.* 头巾
reinforce *v.* 加强；充突

Here's what scientists found: a copper ax, a bow, arrows, a quiver, and a tiny knife. Scientists think that Otzi used the bow and arrows to hunt deer and *ibex*, the knife to clean the animals, the ax to chop firewood, and the quiver to hold the arrows.

Otzi also carried two strips of felt and a small container made of birch bark. Scientists think he may have used the felt as tinder for starting fires and the birch-bark container to carry the felt.

Next to the container was a soft leather pouch with two pieces of *flint*, which were probably used for making tools and for striking sparks to start fire. A four-inch wooden stick with a tip made of deer antler may have been used for sharpening the chunks of flint.

科学家们找到的物品有：铜斧、弓、箭、箭袋还有一把小刀。他们认为弓箭是奥茨用来猎捕鹿和野羊的，刀是用来收拾动物的，斧头是用来砍柴的，箭袋是装箭用的。

奥茨还带了两块毡子和一个桦树皮的小包。科学家们推测，奥茨生火时用毡子来引火。桦树皮包是用来装毡子的。

小包旁边还有一只软皮囊，里面有两个火石石片。大概是用来制作工具和剥树皮生火的。还有一根四英尺的木棍，头是用鹿角做的，也许奥茨用它来打磨石片。

---

ibex *n.* 兆山羊，羱羊（角长而弯曲）　　　　　　　　　　　flint *n.* 火石

Based on this evidence and knowledge of the time period, some scientists theorize that Otzi was hunting and may have accidentally been caught in a crossfire of arrows from other hunters.

Theory 2: Murder for Food

Otzi was not killed accidentally, but was killed *on purpose* in a fierce battle with other hunters.

Other scientists disagree with the accidental death theory. They think that while Otzi was hunting ibex, he *encountered* a group of starving hunters. The hunters desperately needed a kill and did not want Otzi taking the kill from them, so they attacked him, firing arrows. Otzi fired back.

　　基于这些证据和那个时代的特点，一些科学家做出了这样的推断：奥茨当时正在打猎，被其他猎人的箭意外射死了。

　　推断二：图财害命

　　奥茨的死不是意外，他是被其他猎人在一场残酷的打斗中故意杀害的。

　　一些科学家不赞成意外死亡的推断。他们认为奥茨当时正在打野羊，遭遇到一群饥肠辘辘的猎人。这些猎人非常需要获得猎物，不能让奥茨从他们手中拿走猎物，于是他们射出了手中的箭，袭击奥茨。奥茨也进行了回击。

---

on purpose　故意地

encounter　*v.*　遇到

Dr. Tom Loy, director of the Queensland National Institute of Molecular Bioscience, thinks that the Iceman fired two arrows into two of his enemies, pulling his *precious* weapons out of their bodies each time. His theory explains why traces of blood from four other people were found on Otzi's belongings: one from his knife, two from the same *arrowhead*, and a fourth from his coat.

In addition to his attackers shooting arrows at him, they may have attacked him with a knife. Perhaps cuts on Otzi's hands and wrist were from his attempts to defend himself.

Many scientists hold this theory to be true, but some wonder whether Otzi was killed for yet another reason.

昆士兰国家微生物分子研究院的负责人，汤姆卢瓦博士推断，奥茨有两箭射中了敌人，每次他都把他宝贵的箭从敌人的身体中拨出来。他的推断能够解释为什么奥茨的物品上发现了其他四个人的血迹：一处在刀上，两处在同一支箭上，第四处是在他的外衣上。

这些袭击者不仅向他射了箭，还用刀捅了他。也许奥茨手上和腰上的刀伤就是自卫时留下的。

许多科学家都认为这种推断是真的，可是也有一些科学家认为奥茨的死还有其他的解释。

precious *adj.* 宝贵的　　　　　　　　　　arrowhead *n.* 箭头

Theory 3: Murder for Power

Members of his community killed Otzi, a shaman, because he had become too powerful.

Walter Leitner of the Institute for Ancient and Early History at the University of Innsbruck in Austria thinks that the Iceman might have been a shaman. A shaman is a physical and spiritual healer who is thought to have the *capability* of traveling to and from the spirit world for medicine.

When scientists examined Otzi's body, they found a large number of *mysterious* tattoos. The tattoos included stripes, a cross, and small bars. These weren't decorations meant for others to see, for they appeared only on parts of his body that would have been hidden

---

推断三：权力之争

奥茨部落里的人谋害了他，因为他作为巫师，权力太大了。

奥地利因斯布鲁克大学古代和早期历史学院的沃尔特莱特纳认为奥茨可能是位巫师。巫师是救助人们身体和心灵的人，人们相信他能穿越阴阳两界寻找解药。

科学家检查奥茨的身体时，发现了大量的神秘文身。这些文身包括线条、十字和小方块。它们不是那些给别人看的装饰，因为它们都在衣服能盖到的部位。这些刻在冰人脚踝、膝盖上的粗劣文身会是一种古代的针灸

---

capability *n.* 能力　　　　　　　mysterious *adj.* 神秘的

by clothing. Were these 57 crudely carved tattoos found on the Iceman's ankles, knees, and calves an ancient form of *acupuncture*? They were located on, or near, acupuncture points that would be used to treat ailments that Otzi likely suffered from—arthritis and back pain.

Some scientists think that Otzi may have worn jewelry, too. When his body was found, a leather string with a fringe, strung through the two-inch disk made of white stone lay nearby. Could this mysterious object have been worn by a medicine man, like Otzi, as a necklace?

Near Otzi's body, researchers also found two mushrooms on a piece of leather. Scientists know that this kind of mushroom can be used to fight sickness. Was Otzi carrying them as medicine—

方法吗？它们都在或接近关节的位置，有可能是用来治疗奥茨可能患有的疾病——关节炎和后背疼痛的。

有些科学家相信奥茨也可能佩戴饰品。他的尸体被发现的时候，附近有一个带穗的皮链，上面穿着一枚两英寸大小的碟形白色石片。这个神秘的物件会是像奥茨这样的巫师佩戴的项链吗？

研究人员在奥茨的尸体旁边还发现了一串用皮条串的蘑菇。科学家们知道这种蘑菇是用来治病的。这是奥茨带在身上的草药——猎人们需要的

acupuncture *n.* 针灸

something the hunters needed? Was the Iceman really a shaman?

A Secret Kept

These are just a few of the scientific theories about the Iceman. They change when the facts—the clues—change. But sometimes the clues remain the same and the scientists *reinterpret* the facts differently. How do you interpret the facts? What kinds of theories do you have now from the facts about how Otzi may have died?

The Iceman could have died in a vast number of possible ways. For now, though, he is still keeping the true story a secret from us.

药物吗？冰人真的是一名巫师吗？

未解之谜

前面提到的只是关于冰人的几种科学假说。随着发现的物证和线索的变化，推断也不断地发生着变化。不过，好些时候，相同物证的基础上，科学家们也会做出不同的推断。你是怎么看待这些证据的呢？根据现有的证据，你对奥茨之死会做出什么样的推断呢？

导致冰人死亡的原因有很多。现在，对我们来说，当时的真相仍然是个谜。

---

reinterpret *v.* 重新解释

Mysterious Caves

What Are Caves?

A cave is any natural hollow space. Usually when people talk about caves, or *caverns*, they mean there's a hole big enough for someone to use as a doorway into the cave. Usually, too, there's an area in the hollow that sunlight never reaches. Most caves are thousands or millions of years old.

Caves are found underwater, underground, and aboveground. A cave can be tiny, or it can be *enormous*, extending for many miles.

神秘的洞穴

洞穴是什么？

洞穴指的就是天然的空洞。人们通常所说的洞穴或洞窟，指的是能容人通过的大洞。通常，洞穴中空的地方永远也见不到阳光。大多数洞穴都有着千百万年的历史。

无论在水下、地下或者地上，都可能发现洞穴。洞穴可能很小，也可能极大，延伸数英里。美国的每一个州都发现过洞穴，其他国家也是一样。

---

cavern　*n.*　大洞穴　　　　　　　　　　　　　　enormous　*adj.*　巨大的

Caves are found in every state in the United States, and in many other countries.

People are fascinated with caves. Caves can be *magnificently gorgeous*, filled with amazing formations and unusual animals. Adventurous people are lured by the challenge and excitement of seeing places no one may have seen before. Some people even live in caves. Explorers have found clues that show people used caves as homes as long as 30,000 years ago.

In this book, you will learn about the different types of caves and how they form, what formations can be found in a cave, what creatures live within caves, and where some famous caves are found.

人们非常钟爱洞穴。洞穴有可能气派恢宏，并且有着令人称奇的地层结构和稀有动物。探险家们被探寻无人所及之地的挑战欲望和刺激感觉所吸引，有些人干脆住在洞穴里。探索者们已经发现，有证据表明，三万年前人类就以洞穴为家了。

在本书中，你将会看到不同类型的洞穴及其形成过程、在洞穴里可能发现什么样的地层和生物，还有迄今为止发现了哪些著名的洞穴。

---

magnificently *adv.* 宏伟地   gorgeous *adj.* 华丽的

Do You Know?

Caves are ancient, but the land around them is even older. For example, Carlsbad Caverns is less than 10 million years old, while the area of New Mexico surrounding it is 250 million years old!

Where and How Caves Form

Caves form in three places: underground, underwater, and *aboveground*. The way caves form differs according to the type of cave. Nature uses basic tools such as wind and water to shape the earth. All caves form slowly over a very long period of time.

你知道吗?

洞穴非常古老,但是洞穴周围的土地历史更悠长。比如说,卡尔斯巴德洞窟国家公园的历史不足一千万年,但是周围的新墨西哥州已经有两亿五千万年的历史了!

洞穴的位置及形成

有三种地方可以形成洞穴:地下、水下和地上。洞穴形成的方式因洞穴的类型不同而有所差异。大自然运用基本的工具来塑造地球,比如用风或用水。所有的洞穴都是在很长的时期内缓慢形成的。

---

aboveground *adv.* 在地上

Underground Caves

Long ago, shallow seas once covered parts of the Earth that are now land. Billions of tiny *organisms* with shells lived in these seas. As the organisms died and sank to the bottom, their shells piled up on the sea floor. Over many years the shells formed layers of rock called *limestone*. Forces deep below the seas pushed the limestone layers upward, eventually above the seas. Then rainwater seeped into the limestone and mixed with chemicals from *decaying* plants to form a weak acid. The acid seeped into cracks in the limestone. The acid *dissolved*, or ate away, the limestone, enlarging the cracks until a hollow was formed—a limestone cave. How long does it take for the acid to eat away enough limestone to make a cave? It can take well over a million years.

地下洞穴

很久以前，有些地方现在成了陆地，而以前曾经被浅海覆盖。在浅海中，居住着数十亿带壳的微小生物。这些生物死去时沉到海底，它们的壳就在海底一点点堆起来。随着时间流逝，这些壳形成了多层的岩石，叫作"石灰石"。来自海底深处的力量将石灰石层向上推，最终推出海面。然后，雨水渗入石灰石，与腐烂的植物形成的化学物质混合形成了弱酸。弱酸渗入石灰石的裂缝，溶解或腐蚀石灰石，将裂缝不断扩大，直至形成一个空洞——即石灰岩洞。弱酸要花多长时间才能完成腐蚀并形成洞穴呢？也许要花一百万年以上。

organism *n.* 微生物
decay *v.* 腐烂

limestone *n.* 石灰岩
dissolve *v.* 溶解

In areas where a volcano has *erupted*, lava (liquid rock) flows like a stream of hot, thick liquid. The top of the stream cools and hardens to form a roof of rock, while the lava *beneath* continues to flow. After the eruption is over, the lava below the rock roof *drains away* leaving a tube-shaped cave underneath. These are called lava tube caves. Lava tube caves sometimes form a maze of tunnels with branches heading off in many directions.

Underwater Caves

When the Ice Age ended around 40,000 years ago, the sheets of ice covering most of North America and Europe melted causing the

---

在火山喷发的地区，熔岩（液体岩石）像一股又热又厚的液体一样流淌。溪流的顶部冷却下来，硬化成岩石穴顶，而其下方的熔岩仍在继续流动。火山喷发结束后，岩石穴顶下的熔岩渐渐枯竭，形成了管状的洞穴。这样的洞穴就叫作"熔岩管洞穴"。熔岩管洞穴有时会形成一个隧道的迷宫，有很多小路通往不同的方向。

海底洞穴

冰河世纪在四万年以前终结的时候，覆盖北美和欧洲大部分地区的冰

---

erupt *v.* 喷发；爆发　　　　　　　　　　beneath *adv.* 在下面
drain away （使）流走；流出

water level of the oceans to rise, flooding caves beneath hundreds of feet of water. Some underwater caves didn't start above ground, and have always been filled with water. They formed when the weight of the layers of limestone created cracks that became filled with water. Over time the water slowly wore away more of the rock, forming caves.

Aboveground Caves

Water and wind move through cracks in rocks aboveground. Ever so slowly, the wind and water, which carry tiny grains of sand, *grind* away rock and form *erosional* caves. Erosional caves are found in most kinds of rock, but form best in softer rock.

层开始融化，导致海平面上升，并在水下几百英尺的位置形成洞穴。有些海底洞室并不是从地上开始形成的，洞中一直被水填满。在石灰石层的重量造成裂缝导致进水时，就会形成这些洞穴。随着时间一点点过去，水流慢慢冲刷着岩石，直至形成洞穴。

　　地上洞穴

　　通过地面岩石的裂缝，水和风夹带着微小的沙粒慢慢地磨损岩石，形成被腐蚀的洞穴。在大多数种类的岩石中都有被腐蚀的洞穴，但是其形成的最佳环境是在较为柔软的岩石中。

---

grind　*v.* 磨光　　　　　　　　　　　erosional　*adj.* 腐蚀的

The most common caves of ice form in mountain *glaciers* as the glaciers slowly *creep* down the mountainside. Warmer water on the glacier's surface that has been heated by the sun seeps through cracks in the glacier. The warmer water melts ice deep in the glacier and causes glacier caves to form.

Sea caves form wherever ocean waves crash against cliffs. In the United States, sea caves are plentiful in the Pacific Coast states of Washington, Oregon, and California, and also the Na Pali coast of the Hawaiian island of Kauai.

Inside Caves

Since limestone caves are the most common type of caves, we'll

---

最常见的冰川洞是在山丘冰川中形成的，因为融化的冰川会延山边缓缓流下。冰川表面因日照形成的温度较高的水会渗入冰川裂缝。这些水融化了冰川深处的冰，并使其逐渐形成冰川洞。

在海浪冲击着悬崖的地方会形成海蚀洞。在美国，海蚀洞不计其数——无论是在太平洋沿岸的华盛顿州、俄勒冈州、加利福尼亚州，还是在拿帕里海岸夏威夷可爱岛。

洞穴内部

因为石灰岩洞是最常见的洞穴，我们就来近距离看一看石灰岩洞里面

---

glacier *n.* 冰川　　　　　　　　　　creep *v.* 悄悄地缓慢行进

take a closer look inside them. Limestone caves are divided into three main parts: entrances, *twilight* zones, and dark zones.

Entrances may be large or small. They can be a doorway into a mountain, a hole in the ground, or a crack in a *boulder*. Trees and shrubs hide entrances to some caves.

The twilight zone describes any part of the cave into which some sunlight seeps. If you're inside a cave and can see without a flashlight or a lantern, you're in the twilight zone. This zone is usually cool and damp; and you can find animals and bugs living there.

The third cave area is known as the dark zone. As you might guess from the name, there is no light in the dark zone. No plants

---

是什么样子。石灰岩洞分为三部分：入口、弱光带和黑暗带。

入口可大可小，可能是通向山脉的走廊、地面的一处凹陷，或是巨砾的一道裂痕。有时，树木和灌木会遮挡住洞穴的入口。

弱光带指的是洞穴中任何有阳光渗入的地方。如果你身处洞穴之中，没有手电筒或灯光也能看见东西，你就位于弱光带。这一地带通常寒冷潮湿，也可能有各种动物或小虫在此寄居。

洞穴的第三个部分叫作"黑暗带"。从名字就可以得知，黑暗带是漆黑一片。此处没有植物生长，但某些动物和真菌可能会适应这里的生长环

---

twilight *adj.* 模糊的   boulder *n.* 巨石；巨砾

grow there, but some animals and mold have adapted to living in the dark. It is very damp and cool. Water drips *constantly* through the cracks from the ground above.

Cave explorers find amazing and beautiful formations inside caves. These formations hang from the ceiling, rise from the floor, and decorate the walls. They are formed when water drips through the cracks of the rocks above the cave.

Many people are familiar with *stalactites* and *stalagmites*. These form when limestone dissolves in water that drips from the cave ceiling to the floor. As the water *evaporates*, the dissolved limestone builds up, bit by bit, creating stalactites on the ceiling and stalagmites on the floor.

A stalactite, which looks something like a rock icicle, grows only

---

境。此处极其潮湿、阴冷。经常有水从地面的裂缝滴下来。

　　探穴者们在洞穴内部发现了神奇而美丽的洞积物。这些洞积物有的从穴顶垂下，有的从地面崛起，有些则点缀了穴壁。这些都是在水滴穿过洞穴上方的岩石裂缝时形成的。

　　很多人都熟知钟乳石和石笋，有水从穴顶滴到地面，石灰石遇水溶解就形成了钟乳石和石笋。随着水分蒸发，溶解了的石灰石一点点累积起来，就形成了穴顶的钟乳石或地面上的石笋。

　　钟乳石看起来就像一只岩石冰柱，每年只增加2毫米（约为0.08英

---

constantly *adv.* 经常地　　　　　　　　stalactite *n.* 钟乳石
stalagmite *n.* 石笋　　　　　　　　　　evaporate *v.* 蒸发

about 2 millimeters (about 0.08 inches) a year. Stalagmites, which look like upside down icicles, grow at the same speed as stalactites and are often more than 15 meters (50 feet) high and 10 meters (33 feet) wide at their base. They can have rounded, flat, or bowl-shaped tops. Sometimes a stalactite and a stalagmite will join to form a column.

Helpful Hint

If you think of the " c " as standing for " ceiling", it will help you remember that stalactites hang from the top of the cave. If you think of the " g " as standing for " ground", it will help you remember that stalagmites point up from the floor of the cave.

寸）。而石笋看起来像倒立的冰柱，增长速度与钟乳石相同，通常有15米（约为50英尺）高，基座有10米（约为33英尺）宽。其形状多种多样，可能是圆形、平面或者碗形。有时，钟乳石与石笋会彼此相连，形成洞柱。

小贴士

　　如果你认为字母"c"代表"穴顶"，那你就能记住钟乳石是从穴顶吊起来的。如果你认为字母"g"代表"地面"，那你就能记住石笋是从洞穴地面累积而成的。

---

ceiling　*n.* 屋顶

Other cave *formations* are created when water evaporates and leaves behind *minerals*. When water drops slide down the walls, each leaves a bit of limestone behind as the water evaporates. This limestone forms thin sheets that hang from cave ceilings. These are called *draperies* and can become more than 3 meters (10 feet) long. Some draperies are so thin they let light pass through. Draperies are sometimes different colors because minerals from the ground above may add color to water seeping into the cave below.

A soda *straw* is another type of formation found in limestone caves. Like the straw you use to drink a soda, these structures are long and hollow.

A twisty, twirly type of cave formation is called a helictite.

其他洞积物是在水分蒸发后留下矿物质形成的。水滴从穴壁滑下，水分蒸发时总会留下一点石灰石。这些石灰石会形成薄片，从穴顶吊下。这样的薄片叫作"石帘"，长度可达到3米（约为10英尺）。有些石帘会薄到透光。有时，石帘会呈现出不同的颜色，因为地面的矿物质可能会给渗进洞穴的水增添颜色。

"苏打水吸管"是石灰岩洞中发现的另外一种洞积物。这些物质就如同喝汽水时用的吸管一样，是长条的空心管。

有一种弯弯曲曲螺旋形的洞积物叫作"石枝"。

---

formation *n.* 形成物
drapery *n.* 窗帘；织物

mineral *n.* 矿物质
straw *n.* 吸管

A rare formation is called a cave pearl. A pearl may start as a grain of sand that is covered, layer by layer with limestone as the water that contains the mineral dries around the grain of sand. They can be less than an inch in size or more than several inches in *diameter*.

It takes a very long time to build a formation, drop by drop—many thousands of years.

Cave Inhabitants

Creatures, small and large, have made their homes in caves for millions of years. At one time, humans found the enclosed space of a cave was a good place to live. Today, some people still call caves home. In Andalucia, Spain, hundreds of people live in caves, while

---

还有一种很稀有的洞积物叫作"穴珠"。一颗穴珠最初可能只是一粒沙子，当这颗沙粒周围含有矿物质的水分干涸时，沙粒就被石灰石一层层包裹起来。其直径可能不足一英寸，也可能长达几英寸。

洞积物的形成很漫长，一滴接一滴，滴过上千年。

洞穴居民

上百万年来，大大小小的生物都曾以洞穴为家。人们一度觉得与世隔绝的洞穴是居住的理想场所。今天，有些人仍然以洞为家。在西班牙安达路西亚，有数百人居住在洞穴里；而在中国北部，还有上百万人居住在洞

---

diameter *n.* 直径

in northern China there are millions of human cave dwellers. Other countries where people live in caves include Turkey, North Africa, and France.

Many scientists *divide* the animals living inside caves into three groups: the ones who never leave the cave, the ones who live part-time in the cave, and animals who visit caves. The thousands of types of animals who never leave caves can't survive outside them. These animals have adapted to survive in the dark. They include some kinds of millipedes, cave spiders, crickets, beetles, spiders, centipedes, crawfish, *salamanders*, and fish. They may be blind and may not have eyes. They are often colorless.

穴里。在土耳其、北非和法国等地，也有人居住在洞穴里。

许多科学家将住在洞穴里的动物分为三类：从不离洞的动物、有时离洞的动物和偶尔来访的动物。那些从不离洞的动物包含数千个物种，一旦离洞便无法存活。这些动物已经适应了在黑暗中生存，其中包括不同种类的百足虫、洞穴蜘蛛、蟋蟀、甲虫、蜘蛛、蜈蚣、小龙虾、蝾螈和鱼类。这些生物可能没有视觉，甚至没有眼睛。通常，它们都是无色的。

---

divide *v.* 分发；分开　　　　salamander *n.* 蝾螈（两栖动物，形似蜥蜴）

Animals that live both inside and outside caves can survive in either place. Examples of these include some beetles, land crayfish, millipedes, centipedes, and some salamanders.

Other animals visit caves for shelter, to rest, or to hunt for food, but spend most of their time outside the cave. This group includes bats, bears, foxes, pack rats, snakes, raccoons, moths, groundhogs, vultures, and crickets.

Exploring Caves

People who explore caves are called spelunkers. Why do spelunkers go into caves? Some do it for adventure and the *physical* challenge of climbing down ropes, crawling through tiny tunnels,

---

在洞内、洞外两处生活的动物在洞内外都能存活。这一类动物包括某些种类的甲虫、小龙虾、百足虫、蜈蚣和蝾螈。

其他的动物只是偶尔来到洞穴，为了躲避、休息或觅食，但大部分时间里，他们是在洞穴外生活的。这种动物包括蝙蝠、熊、狐狸、狐尾大林鼠、蛇、浣熊、飞蛾、土拨鼠、秃鹰和蟋蟀。

探索洞穴

探索洞穴的人被称为"探穴者"。探穴者们为什么要进入洞穴呢？有些人是为了冒险，挑战身体极限。他们可以顺绳而下，爬行于狭窄的隧

---

physical *adj.* 身体的

and exploring deeper regions of the Earth. Other spelunkers like discovering places possibly seen by no one else on Earth. Scientists enter caves to learn more about the Earth.

Do You Know?

In 1940, four boys accidentally discovered one of the most famous art caves, France's Lascaux Cave. They **squeezed** *into a small hole, entering a large cavern with beautiful paintings of deer and bulls. Luckily, the boys were not hurt, but entering a cave without an experienced cave explorer or guide is a dangerous idea. Later, one of the boys became the cave's main guide.*

道，或者探索地球上更深的地方。其他的探穴者喜欢探索一些也许从来没有人发现的地方。科学家们进入洞穴是为了知道更多关于地球的信息。

你知道吗？

1940年，有4个男孩子无意中发现了最著名的艺术洞穴之一——法国拉斯科洞穴。几个孩子挤进一个小洞，进入了一个大型洞穴，里面有漂亮的麋鹿和公牛壁画。幸运的是，他们没有受伤，但是没有有经验的探穴人或导游引导而进入洞穴是很危险的。后来，其中的一个男孩子成了这个洞穴的主要导游。

squeeze *v.* 挤

A cave is exciting and exotic, and it can definitely be dangerous. So if you plan to visit a cave, take a guided tour to avoid getting hurt. The guide can explain many wonders to be found inside a cave, and safely get you in and out. They can keep you from damaging the cave.

A cave has taken millions of years to form and is full of *delicate* formations. A visitor can damage it without thinking. *Thoughtless* cave guests have broken off stalactite tips as souvenirs, destroying in a second something that may have taken 40,000 years to form.

People have also thrown coins in underground pools, polluting

---

洞穴很令人兴奋，别有风情，但是洞穴也很危险。所以如果你计划参观洞穴，一定要跟着导游走，以免受伤。导游会解释洞穴内部许多值得探索的奇妙之处，也能保证你安全地进出洞穴。他们也能保护洞穴免遭意外破坏。

形成一个洞穴需要上百万年的时间，其内部构造更是异彩纷呈。一些粗心的洞穴游客会折断钟乳石尖作为纪念物，一瞬间就毁掉了4万年累积的成果。

人们还在地下池里投硬币，污染了池子，也有人在洞穴里留下了垃

---

delicate *adj.* 精美的   thoughtless *adj.* 粗心大意的

them, or left trash in caves. Caves lie so close to natural water *reservoirs* that when we pollute caves, we can also pollute drinking water. When you visit a cave, you should leave a cave exactly as you found it.

Experienced cave explorers *equip* themselves with helmets, flashlights, warm clothing, and knee pads. They may descend into the cave on a rope. As the spelunkers go deeper, their eyes must adjust to the darkness. They may have to wriggle through a tiny tunnel. In the cave, they hear water drip-drip-dripping, but no other sound. The only light is the glow of their flashlights.

圾。洞穴与天然水库距离非常近，这样当洞穴被污染时，饮用水也被污染了。当游客参观洞穴时，不应该对洞穴造成任何改变。

有经验的探穴者会自备头盔、手电筒、保暖的衣服和护膝。他们会顺着绳子进入洞穴。当探穴者降到较深处，他们的眼睛必须适应黑暗。他们需要在狭窄的隧道内蜿蜒前进。在洞穴里，他们可以听到水滴的声音，但是没有任何其他的声音。而唯一的光源就是他们手电筒的光。

---

reservoir *n.* 水库   equip *v.* 配备；装备

Do You Know?

Caves are too deep to be affected by seasons. Cave temperatures tend to be between 24 degrees C (75°F) and 1 degrees C (30°F).

Famous Caves

There are caves throughout the world known for one or more *outstanding* features. One of the most *renowned* caves is the Chauvet Cave in France. It was discovered in 1994, and contains more than 300 of the world's oldest paintings— approximately 30,000 years old. The paintings include horses, lions, bears, and *rhinoceroses*.

Mexico's Cheve Cave is famous for being one of the deepest

你知道吗?

洞穴的位置很深，不会因四季的交替而变化。洞穴的温度通常在1℃（30°F）到24℃（75°F）之间。

著名洞穴

世界上有很多著名的洞穴，特点各不相同。其中最著名的洞穴之一是法国的萧韦岩洞。这座洞穴是1994年发现的，穴内有三百多幅世界上最古老的绘画作品——其历史约有三万年。图画内容包括马、狮子、熊和犀牛等。

outstanding *adj.* 显著的　　　　　renowned *adj.* 有名的
rhinoceros *n.* 犀牛

cave systems in the world. The deepest tunnels may be more than 2,000 meters (6,500 feet) below the surface. The world's largest known natural cave *chamber* is Sarawak Chamber in Asia's Sarawak, Borneo. The world's largest known cave passage, Deer Cave, is also located in the network of caves in Sarawak, Borneo.

The United States claims some famous caves, too. Mammoth Cave in Kentucky contains more than 300 miles (482.08 km) of known passageways, making it the largest known cave system in the world. Carlsbad Caverns in New Mexico is a national *monument* with more than 80 known caves in the system. Carlsbad's magnificent Big Room is the seventh largest known cave in the world. It measures

墨西哥的奇夫洞穴是以世界上最深的洞穴而闻名的。其中最深的隧道达到了地面以下2000米（约为6500英尺）。世界上最大的已知天然洞室是位于亚洲的婆罗洲沙捞越的"沙捞越洞"。世界上最大的已知洞穴通道是"鹿洞"，鹿洞同样位于婆罗洲沙捞越的大片洞穴之中。

美国也拥有一些著名的洞穴。肯塔基州的猛犸洞共有300多英里（482.08公里）长的通道，使这一洞穴成为世界已知的最大洞穴体系。新墨西哥州的卡尔斯巴德洞穴也是美国的历史遗迹，目前已知其中有80多个洞室。卡尔斯巴德壮观的"大房间"是全球第七大已知洞穴。此洞长

chamber *n.* 房间；室　　　　monument *n.* 遗迹

1,800 feet (548.64 meters) long, as much as 1,100 feet (335.28 m) wide, and 255 feet (77.72 m) deep.

Conclusion

The world of caves is fascinating. Where else on Earth can you find unexplored land, discover *otherworldly* formations, and see artwork from thousands and thousands of years ago? As long as we treat them respectfully, we can continue to experience the wonder of caves *indefinitely*.

达1800英尺（548.64米），宽达1100英尺（335.28米），深达255英尺（77.72米）。

小结

洞穴的世界引人入胜。在其他什么地方你还能找到这样的未开发之地，发现这样超凡脱俗的天然宝物，观赏这样经成千上万年累积而成的艺术杰作呢？只要我们带着敬畏之心去欣赏洞穴，我们就越来越能够体验到洞穴艺术的无限精妙。

---

otherworldly *adj.* 超世俗的　　　　　　　　indefinitely *adv.* 无限地

07

Yee Haw! The Real Lives of the Cowboys

Introduction

Mention the word *cowboy*, and a picture quickly comes to mind: a tough man in boots and a hat who is fast with his gun. While this romantic image is known around the world, the real cowboys were very different. Cowboys didn't spend their time rescuing *maidens* or getting in shootouts. They were workers who

---

呦嗬！牛仔的真实生活

简介

每当提到牛仔这个词，这样一幅图画便会浮现在脑海：一个身材高大健壮结实的牛仔，头戴宽边帽，脚蹬长筒靴，胯边垂着火筒枪，当匪徒一个个应声倒地时，若无其事地骑马飞驰而去。虽然这个浪漫的影像为全世界所熟知，但现实生活中的牛仔却是非常不一样的。牛仔并不会去花时间营救一名少女或卷入一场枪战。他们仅仅是从事艰苦、危

---

cowboy *n.* 牛仔　　　　　　　　　　maiden *n.* 少女

performed a tough, dangerous, and exhausting job. It was this difficult, lonely work that first made cowboys icons of the American West.

The Cowboy Era Begins

In the 1860s, enormous cattle *ranches* spread over large areas of western North America. Since so few people lived on the huge plains of Texas, Wyoming, Utah, and Montana, ranchers let their cattle wander over the land. The cows grew fat and healthy on the wild grass. But most of the major *slaughterhouses* and cattle markets were in northern and eastern cities. The ranchers needed some way to round up thousands of cows and take them to railroad stations to get them to market. Before the railroad spread to the western states, the only way to do this was on *horseback*.

险并且劳累的工作者。也正是这种艰苦寂寞的工作使牛仔成了美国西部的标志。

牛仔时代开始了

19世纪60年代，大量的牧场遍布了北美西部的大片地区。因为在得克萨斯州、怀俄明州、犹他州和蒙大拿州的广阔平原上，人迹罕至，因此牧场经营者让他们的牛在这片土地上任意游荡。母牛靠这里的野草长得又肥又壮。但大部分主要屠宰场和牛市都集中在北部和东部城市，因此牧场主需要想出一些办法将上千头牛集中到一起并将其送到铁路车站进行市场交易。在铁路延伸到西部之前，唯一的办法就是骑马。

---

ranch *n.* 牧场；大农场

slaughterhouse *n.* 屠宰场

horseback *n.* 马背

At the same time, many young men had lost their jobs. The U.S. Civil War left soldiers and freed slaves with few *opportunities*. People of Mexican *descent* and Native Americans were forced west as settlers moved in. Many of these out-of-work young men went to the western ranches. There was plenty of land and lots of work to be done there.

Ranchers hired strong men and taught them to handle horses. They sent them onto the range to round up the cattle and march them to railroad stations on the northern and eastern plains. Leading these cattle drives was the original work of cowboys. More than one quarter of American cowboys were Hispanic, Native American, or African-American.

与此同时，很多年轻人失去了工作。美国内战给士兵和解放的奴隶几乎没有留下就业的机会。墨西哥人口数量减少了，随着殖民者的迁入，美洲原住民被迫向西迁移。很多失业青年来到了西部的牧场。这里有大片的土地，也有很多工作让他们做。

牧场主雇用强壮的男子并教他们怎样侍弄马匹。牧场主把他们派到牧场，让他们把牛集中到一起然后赶到北部和东部平原的铁路站。押送牛群是牛仔最原始的工作。超过四分之一的美国牛仔是西班牙裔，美洲原住民，或者非裔美国人。

opportunity *n.* 机会

descent *n.* 血统；家世

The first cowboys were Mexicans who called themselves *vaqueros*. They were experienced horse handlers who taught the newcomers how to work with cattle and horses. They invented much of the familiar equipment and clothing that cowboys used, including the *lasso*, the cowboy hat (a form of the sombrero), and leather chaps. Chaps are leg coverings that protected cowboys from *cactuses* and other spiny plants. The vaqueros were often the ones who captured and *tamed* mustangs, or wild horses, for other cowboys to ride. Mustangs were nearly impossible to control until after the skilled vaqueros had tamed them. The vaqueros trained both cowboys and horses for the grueling cattle drive.

最早的牛仔是墨西哥人，他们称自己为牧者。他们是有经验的驯马师，并教授新来者如何驯服牛马。他们发明了很多牛仔使用的常见装备和服装，包括套索、牛仔帽（一种宽边帽）以及皮套裤。皮套裤是一种保护牛仔不受仙人掌或其他多刺植物伤害的腿套。牧者经常将捕获的野马驯服后供其他牛仔骑行。除非熟练的牧者将其驯服，否则野马几乎是不可能控制的。牧者会为这种繁复而累人的押送牛群工作，对牛仔和马匹进行培训和训练。

vaquero *n.* 牧者　　　　　　　lasso *n.* 套索
cactus *n.* 仙人掌　　　　　　 tame *v.* 驯服

Do You Know?

Many cowboy terms come from Spanish words invented by the vaqueros.

Some common examples are:

Chaps *from the Spanish word chaparejos*

Rodeo *from the Spanish word meaning "to surround"*

Lariat *a cowboy's rope, from the Spanish word la reata*

Mustang *from the Spanish word mustaños*

Buckaroo *a form of the word vaquero*

The Cattle Drive

The Roundup

The cowboys' first task was to go out from the ranch house and

---

你知道吗？

许多牛仔术语来自由牧者发明的西班牙语词汇。下面是一些普通的例子：

皮套裤 来自西班牙语单词chaparejos（皮裤）
围场 来自西班牙语单词，意思是"包围"
套索 牛仔用的绳子，来自西班牙语单词 la reata（套索）
野马 来自西班牙语单词mustaños
牛仔 单词vaquero（牧者）的一种形式

押送牛群
赶拢
牛仔的第一项任务就是走出牧场主低矮的平房把要驱赶的牛群集中到

---

surround *v.* 包围

gather all the cattle for the drive. The ranchers had branded their cattle, or burned a pattern into their skin, so they could tell whose cow was whose. This was necessary because the cattle were scattered over miles and mixed in with other herds. The cowboys *herded* the cattle onto the ranch, *sorted* them, branded any new calves, and prepared for the long trek ahead.

On the Trail

About 2,500 cattle and 15 to 20 cowboys went on a typical cattle drive. This included the trail boss, who was the highest-paid member of the crew. The trail boss was the leader of the drive. He was responsible for deciding the price of the cattle at the railroad station.

一起。牧场主在他们自己的牛上打上烙印，或在其外皮上烙上图案，这样他们就能分得清这些牛属于谁了。这是必要的，因为牧场主饲养的牛分散到了几英里之外，会与其他牛群混合到一起。牛仔将牛群放牧到牧场上，对其进行分类，将所有的小牛打上烙印，为将来的艰苦跋涉作准备。

征途

在这种典型的押送牛群的过程中，15到20名牛仔一次要押送约2,500头牛。领队是负责押送牛群的牛仔中报酬最高的人，他是押送牛群过程中的总指挥。领队负责在铁路站确定牛的价格。厨师，通常也在押送过程中

---

herd *v.* 把……赶在一起　　　　　　sort *v.* 整理；把……分类

The cook, who often served as the drive's doctor, drove a chuck *wagon* filled with food, supplies, medicine, and other goods. Even though he did not handle cows or horses, the cook was a highly respected member of the crew. He was often African-American. A *wrangler*, usually a teenage boy, kept track of the extra horses. Cowboys needed to switch horses when the horses became tired, sick, or hurt.

For the first few days, the cowboys drove the cattle hard, trying to get them away from familiar land. The cattle were not used to being in a large group, and they tried to run back to their old *pastures*. But after a few days, the pace relaxed. Cows were sold by the pound, and going too fast would make them lose weight. New cowboys, or

担任医生，驾驶装满食物、补给品、药品和其他货物的流动炊事车。尽管厨师不侍弄牛群或马匹，但他在队伍中却是德高望重的。厨师通常是非裔美国人。牧马人通常是十几岁的青少年，他负责照顾那些备用的马匹。当马匹疲劳、生病或受伤的时候，牛仔就需要换马了。

　　头几天的时间里，牛仔驱赶牛群是很困难的，他们必须努力让牛群远离它们熟悉的土地。牛群还不习惯成群结队，因此它们试图跑回它们熟悉的牧场。但几天以后，它们的步伐开始放缓。牛是按磅出售的，行进得太快会使它们的重量减轻。新手守在牛群后面，这算是最糟糕的地方了。牛

wagon *n.* 四轮运货马车　　　　　　　　　　　wrangler *n.* 牧马人
pasture *n.* 牧场

greenhorns, rode in the back. This was the worst place to be. The cows kicked up lots of dust and left piles of smelly dung behind. Bandanas came in handy keeping dust and bad smells away from the cowboy's mouth and nose.

The trail boss and the cook rode ahead of the herd, searching for the next night's *campsite*. In the dry west, water sources were very important. The cook and trail boss had to be excellent *navigators* in order to find them. The cook set up camp and began dinner while the cattle followed behind. In a day's ride, the group could travel 15 to 20 miles (24–32 km). Cowboys often rode 16 hours a day through rain, storms, and terrible heat.

群踢起大量的灰尘，并且把成堆难闻的牛粪丢在后面。大手帕在这派上了用场，它能够让牛仔的嘴和鼻子远离灰尘和难闻的气味。

领队和厨师在牛群前面骑行寻找下一夜的露营地。在干燥的西部，水源是非常重要的。为了能够找到水源，厨师和领队必须是出色的引路人。当牛群还跟在后面的时候，厨师就得在前面扎好营地、准备好晚餐。在一天的骑行中，队伍可以行进15至20英里（24至32公里）。牛仔经常在狂风暴雨或极端炎热的天气中一天骑行16个小时。

campsite *n.* 野营地　　　　　navigator *n.* 导航员

The cowboys' hats kept sun and rain off their faces. Tough cowboy boots sat comfortably in the *stirrups* and protected the cowboy's ankles from biting insects, scorpions, and snakes. The boots had pointed toes, so if a cowboy fell off his horse, he could slip his foot out of the stirrup before he was *trampled*.

At night, at least two cowboys always stood guard. They even ate dinner in shifts so that someone could always watch the cattle. Guards rode their horses around the herd, making sure no cows ran away. They watched for wild animals, such as wolves or coyotes, and for any human thieves or attackers. They often sang quiet, lonesome songs under the stars in order to keep the cows calm. The last late-night watch would wake the cook, who would begin breakfast, and the drive would move again.

　　牛仔的帽子可以遮光挡雨。结实的牛仔靴可以舒服地踩在马镫上，也能够使牛仔的踝部不受昆虫，蝎子和蛇的叮咬。牛仔靴是尖头的，所以如果牛仔从马上摔下来的话，在他受伤之前，他可以把脚从马镫中滑出。

　　夜晚，至少有两名牛仔时刻站岗。他们甚至轮班吃饭以保证能有人一直看着牛群。为了确保没有牛跑掉，守卫骑着马在牛群周围巡逻。他们要留心野兽，如狼或土狼，也留心小偷和袭击者。为了让牛群保持安静，他们经常在星空下唱着安静寂寞的歌曲。最后一班岗将会叫醒厨师，因为他要为大家准备早餐，开始新的征程了。

---

stirrup *n.* 马镫

trample *v.* 伤害；践踏

Cowboy food wasn't much to crow about; any supplies had to be cheap and *nonperishable*. The most common foods were beans, hotcakes and biscuits (which the cook made fresh daily), canned fruit, bacon, and strong coffee. Since the cowboys were exercising all day, they ate quite a lot and kept the cook busy. The cook often hunted and fished to add to the cowboys' diet.

The Market

A cattle drive usually lasted two to three months, seven days a week. At the end of the drive, the cowboys led the cattle through the streets of a railroad town and loaded them on trains *bound* north and east. Afterward, the cowboys got much-needed baths and haircuts.

　　牛仔的食物没什么特别的。任何补给必须是廉价不易坏的。最常见的食物包括豆子、烤饼和饼干（厨师每天都做新鲜的）、水果罐头、培根还有浓咖啡。因为牛仔整天运动，所以他们吃得很多，这让厨师非常忙碌。厨师经常会去打猎、捕鱼来增加牛仔的食谱。

　　集市

　　押送牛群通常会持续两三个月，一周七天连续不停。在押送结束的时候，牛仔带领着牛群穿过铁路城镇的街道，将它们装上发往北部和东部的火车。然后，他们迫切需要洗洗澡、理理发。他们去酒吧、舞厅和剧院放

---

nonperishable adj. 不易损坏的　　　　　　　　bound adj. 准备前往（某地）

They relaxed in *saloons*, dance halls, and theaters, and bought more supplies before heading home. The ride back often went much faster than the drive. The cowboys could get good nights' sleep under the stars and spend their extra time hunting and fishing. Once back in ranch land, they would begin looking to get hired on the next drive.

Stampede! And Other Dangers

Cows are herd animals, which means they travel in large groups for protection. Wild herd animals, such as buffalo and wildebeest, have one defense against predators and other dangers: the stampede. As a group, they run at top speed, trampling everything

松身体，在回家之前买更多的补给品。返程通常要比押送快很多。牛仔可以在星空下睡上一个好觉，而且有额外的时间打猎和捕鱼。一旦回到了牧场，他们就开始盼望在下一次押送中得到雇用。

惊逃以及其他危险

牛是群体动物，也就是说为了得到保护，它们成群结队地行进。野生群体动物，如水牛、牛羚，在遇到食肉动物或其他危险的时候有一种防御措施：惊逃。最为一个群体，它们全速奔跑，在它们逃跑的过程中肆意地

saloon *n.* 酒吧

in their path in hopes of *outrunning*, hurting, or confusing their *predators*. Stampedes were a cowboy's biggest fear.

While on the trail, the cows were nervous and *stressed*. A rattlesnake, lightning, or any sudden loud noise could startle the cattle and cause a stampede. Thousands of cattle would run forward at once. The cows moved so quickly that they often hurt or killed themselves by falling off cliffs, drowning in rivers, or catching their legs in holes. Often, stampedes happened at night when the cowboys couldn't see the cows or any dangers they might run into. The only way to stop a stampede was by circling the cattle.

践踏，希望能甩开、撞伤或迷惑这些食肉动物。牛仔最害怕的就是它们发生惊逃。

由于牛的胆子很小，因此在路上，响尾蛇、闪电，或任何突然的声响都可能惊吓到牛群并引起它们惊逃，数以千计的牛会立刻向前奔跑。牛群跑得非常快，以至于它们经常跌落悬崖、溺水或陷入陷阱而受伤甚至死亡。通常，惊逃发生在牛仔看不见牛群或他们可能遭遇危险的夜晚。阻止惊逃的唯一方法是环骑。

---

outrun *v.* 跑得比……快   predator *n.* 食肉动物
stressed *adj.* 紧张的

Do You Know?

Native Americans often owned their own cattle ranches. During the time of the cowboys, all of what is now Oklahoma was American Indian **territory**. *The Native Americans didn't like having someone else's cattle feeding on grass that should have been for their own cows. If the cattle drives wished to cross their land, the Native Americans charged a* **toll** *of ten cents for each cow. Sometimes, if the trail boss refused to pay, the Native Americans might sneak up on the drive during the night and start a stampede.*

The most experienced cowboys would leap on the strongest,

你知道吗？

美洲原住民通常有他们自己的牛场。在牛仔时代，现今的整个俄克拉荷马州都是美国印第安人的领地。美洲原住民不喜欢让别人的牛吃本该让他们自己牛群吃的草。如押送牛群要从他们的领地经过，美洲原住民要为每头牛收取10美分的通行费。有时，如果领队拒绝支付通行费，美洲原住民会在夜晚偷偷接近牛群使牛群发生惊逃。

经验最丰富的牛仔会骑在最强壮、速度最快的马上紧紧围着牛群飞

territory *n.* 领土　　　　　　　　　　　toll *n.* （桥梁、通道的）通行费

fastest horses. They would ride closely alongside the herd and force the cows to crowd together by shouting and *bumping* against them. They made the cows on the outside run in a circle, and the cows on the inside would follow. Once they were running in a circle, the cattle would *eventually* get tired and stop.

This was not an easy task. A cow could knock a cowboy off his horse and trample or gore him. The horse itself could get scared and run off. If stampedes happened at night, the cowboys' horses were *vulnerable* to the same cliffs, rivers, and holes as the cattle were. And sometimes, the cows refused to go into a circle. Instead, they ran off in all directions. The cattle drive was forced to wait while the

---

驰，通过呼喊和撞击牛群迫使他们聚到一起。他们使外面的牛群跑成一圈，然后里面的牛群会跟着跑成一圈。一旦牛群跑成一圈，他们最终会由于疲倦而停下来。

这并不是一项简单的任务。牛可能将牛仔从马上撞下来然后踩伤或刺伤牛仔。马匹本身也会受到惊吓而逃跑。如果夜晚发生了惊逃，牛仔的马匹可能会受到像牛群一样的伤害，跌落悬崖，溺水或陷入陷阱。有时候，牛群会拒绝跑成一圈，相反，他们跑向四面八方。当牛仔经过荒野的时候，由于要将每头离群的牛召集回来，有时押送工作不得不停下来。

---

bump *v.* 碰撞　　　　　　　　　　　eventually *adv.* 最终
vulnerable *adj.* 易受……伤害的

cowboys rode across the wilderness, gathering up every stray cow.

River crossings were also dangerous. Cows could drown or become caught in deep sand. Rattlesnakes and scorpions threatened the lives of both cattle and cowboys. The cowboys were miles from any hospital to treat injuries and *infections*. Cattle and horse rustlers were a common and hated danger of the drive. The West also had dangerous weather, including flash floods, tornadoes, and lightning. Cowboys even developed a *superstition* about lightning striking white horses. The western U.S. can also become harshly cold, even in the summertime. Records show that many cowboys died of *pneumonia* and *hypothermia*.

渡河也是很危险的。牛群可能被淹死或陷入河沙中。响尾蛇和蝎子不仅对牛群，而且对牛仔的生命也构成了威胁。牛仔距离处理伤口和感染的医院有几英里远。偷牛贼是押送中一种常见并让人憎恶的危险因素。美国西部还有天气带来的危险，如山洪暴发、龙卷风，还有闪电。牛仔甚至产生了闪电袭击白马的迷信。即使是在夏季，美国西部也可能变得异常寒冷。记录显示很多牛仔死于肺炎和低体温症。

infection *n.* 感染　　　　　　　superstition *n.* 迷信
pneumonia *n.* 肺炎　　　　　　hypothermia *n.* 体温过低

The End of the Era

Though cowboys became famous for their bravery, the need for cattle drives didn't last long. The railroad expanded rapidly. Eventually, the trains came to Texas, Colorado, and other ranch states. Ranchers no longer needed to drive their cattle hundreds of miles to distant stations. After the invention of *barbed* wire, ranchers also began fencing in their land. Rounding up cows was no longer necessary. Even if the cowboys wanted to continue the cattle drives, the fences would block their way.

牛仔时代的终结

尽管牛仔因其勇敢无畏而著称，但押送牛群的需求并没有持续多长时间。铁路迅速扩张，最终，火车开到了得克萨斯、科罗拉多和其他有牧场的州。牧场主不再需要将他们的牛群赶往数百英里以外遥远的车站了。铁丝网发明以后，牧场主也开始在他们的牧场围栅栏。他们不再需要聚拢牛群了。即使牛仔希望能够继续押送牛群，但这些栅栏成了他们的羁绊。

---

barbed *adj.* 有刺的

Do You Know?

Texas cattle in the 1860s were an especially mean breed called Texas longhorns. Their huge horns could span nine feet (2.7 m). During the Civil War when ranchers were away, the cows had run wild. Some of the longhorns had never seen a human being before, and they often attacked and killed cowboys and their horses.

While longhorns were mean, they weren't very tough when it came to disease or weather. Longhorns carried a disease called "Texas fever" that could spread to other cattle. An **extremely** harsh winter in 1886 froze thousands of longhorns to death. This tragedy was one of the things that helped end the cowboy **era**.

你知道吗？

19世纪60年代，得克萨斯牛非常难以驯服，人们称这里的牛为得克萨斯长角牛。他们巨大的牛角跨度可达9英尺（2.7米）。内战期间，牧场主都离开了，牛群失去了控制。一些长角牛此前从未见到过人类，它们经常攻击甚至杀死牛仔和他们的马匹。

尽管长角牛难以驯服，但遇到疾病和坏天气的时候，它们并不是非常强壮。长角牛携带一种叫作"得克萨斯热"的疾病，这种疾病可以传播给其他的牛。1886年的一场寒冬冻死了数以千头的长角牛。这场悲剧成为了加速牛仔时代终结的其中一个因素。

---

extremely *adv.* 非常

era *n.* 时代

But the cowboy life was far from over. Just as real cowboys were finding themselves out of work, Buffalo Bill Cody began his Wild West show. Cowboys were hired to show their riding and roping skills to crowds across the United States and in Europe. Annie Oakley, one of the most famous cowgirls, was a star of the Wild West show. It was this show that really created the *legend* of the American cowboy. The show included plays and acts that portrayed cowboys as rough and tough *gunslingers*, even though few had carried guns in real life. They made cowboy fashion, including jeans, vests, hats, and boots, popular with people throughout the world.

Long after the American West became settled, Western movies

　　但牛仔生活却远未结束。就当现实生活中的牛仔发现他们已经失业的时候，水牛比尔科迪开始了他的西大荒演出。牛仔被雇用在整个美国和欧洲向人们表演他们的骑术和绳索技艺。安妮·奥克利，最著名的女牛仔之一，是西大荒演出的明星。是西大荒演出真正创造了美国牛仔的传奇。演出包括戏剧和表演，这里把牛仔描绘成了高大强壮的枪手——尽管在现实生活中牛仔很少持枪。演出使牛仔变得时髦，牛仔裤、背心、牛仔帽，还有牛仔靴受到了全世界人们的欢迎。

　　人们在美国西部定居很长时间以后，美国西部电影开始蓬勃发展。

---

legend n. 传奇　　　　　　　　　　gunslinger n. 枪手；杀手

exploded in *popularity*. During the 1950s and 1960s, cowboy movies, television shows, toys, and games were everywhere. *The Lone Ranger* and *Bonanza* became popular TV shows. Children played "cowboys and Indians" in schoolyards, even though in the real West, Native Americans often were cowboys. Today, you can see cowboy boots and hats in Tokyo and Paris as well as Texas. The cowboy has become little more than an image used to sell jeans, trucks, and cigarettes. But that image wouldn't exist without the hard work and bravery of the real cowboys of the North American West.

二十世纪五六十年代，牛仔电影、电视节目、玩具，还有游戏遍布各地。《独行侠》和《大淘金》成了受欢迎的电视节目。孩子们在操场玩"牛仔和印第安人"的游戏——即使在现实中的美国西部，通常美洲原住民本身就是牛仔。现如今，你可以像在得克萨斯一样在东京和巴黎看到牛仔靴和牛仔帽。牛仔差不多成了销售牛仔裤、卡车，还有香烟的形象代言人。但如果没有北美西部真正牛仔的勤勤恳恳和英勇无畏，这种形象如何得以存在？

explode *v.* 激增   popularity *n.* 流行